Monogram of the entire alphabet. (From Demengeot, *Dictionnaire du Chiffre-monogramme*)

DOVER *Pictorial Archive* SERIES

Monograms and Alphabetic Devices

EDITED BY

HAYWARD AND BLANCHE CIRKER

DOVER PUBLICATIONS, INC.

NEW YORK

This Dover edition, first published in 1970, contains the
following material:
Unabridged republication of the plates for *Dictionnaire
du Chiffre-monogramme dans les Styles Moyen-age et
Renaissance et Couronnes nobiliaires universelles* by
Charles Demengeot, published by the author, Paris, 1881.
Unabridged republication of *Monograms and Ciphers*
by H. Renoir, published by A. Fullarton and Company, Lon-
don and Edinburgh, 1870-74.
Unabridged republication of *Knight's New Book of
Seven Hundred & Fifty Eight Plain, Ornamented & Re-
versed Cyphers,* published by F. Knight, London, 1830.
Unabridged republication of *Monograms in Three and
Four Letters* by J. Gordon Smith, published by Thomas C.
Jack London [n.d.].

Standard Book Number: 486-22330-2
Library of Congress Catalog Card Number: 74-78827

Manufactured in the United States of America
Dover Publications, Inc.
180 Varick Street
New York, N. Y. 10014

Contents

Dictionnaire du Chiffre-monogramme   By CH. DEMENGEOT   1

Monograms and Ciphers   By H. RENOIR   39

New Book of Seven Hundred & Fifty Eight Plain, Ornamented & Reversed Cyphers   By F. KNIGHT   109

Monograms in Three and Four Letters   By J. GORDON SMITH   141

Index of Names and Devices   215

Index of Monograms and Ciphers   219

Dictionnaire du Chiffre-monogramme

BY CH. DEMENGEOT

Dictionaire
du
Chiffre-Monogramme
DANS LES STYLES MOYEN-AGE, ET RENAISSANCE
&
Couronnes Nobiliaires
Universelles.

34

LANCHES GRAVÉES AU BURIN,
accompagnées d'un texte historique sur les
Chiffres Monogrammes et Couronnes
Depuis l'Antiqvite, jusqu'à nos jovrs :

Composition, Gravure et Texte, par

CHARLES DEMENGEOT
Graveur Héraldiste.

A Paris.

Chez Ch. DEMENGEOT
Graveur
48. Rue de La Tour d'Auvergne.

Chez Charles JULIOT
Libraire
22 Rue des Ecoles.

1881

Composé et Ecrit par C. DEMENGEOT, et I. LANCELEVÉE.

Photogravure P. DUJARDIN.

A · A

A · B

A · C

A · D

A · E

A · F

Couronne du St. Empire.

ALICE

A · G

Couronne Imple de Russie.

A · H

A · I

A · J

A · K

A · L

A · M

A · N

A · O

A · P

A · Q

A · R

ALBERT
COURONNE DE DUC

A · S

A · T

A · U

A · V

A · W

A · X

A · Y

A · Z

B · B

C.^{nne} de CHARLEMAGNE
VIIIe. Siècle

C.^{nne} de CHARLES LE CHAUVE
IXe. Siècle

B · B

B · C

B · D

B · E

AMÉLIE

B · F

B · G

B · H

B · I

B · J

B · K

B · L

B · M

B · N

B · O

B · P

B · Q

B · R

BENOIT
COUR. de NOBLESSE

B · S

B · T

B · U

B · V

B · W

B · X

C · C

B · Y

C · D

B · Z

C · E

C · F

C · G

BERTHE
COUR. de VICOMTE

C · H

C · I

C · J

C · K

C · L

C · M

C·N

COURONNE D'EUDES D'AQUITAINE

C·O

COURONNE DE LOUIS IX

C·P

VII? Siècle.

XIII? Siècle.

C·Q

C·R

CATHERINE

C·S

C·T

C·U

C·V

C·W

C·X

C·Y

Ç·Z

D·F

D·E

D·H

D·I

D·J

D·K

D·L

D·M

D·N

D·O

D·P

D·Q

D·R

D·S

D·T

D·U

D·V
COURᴺᴺᴱ ROYALE DE FRANCE.

DAVID
COURONNE DE FANTAISIE.

D·W
COURONNE DAUPHINALE.

D·X

D·Y

D·Z

E

E·F

E G

E H

E I

E J

E M

E K

E L

E N

E O

E P

E Q

E R

E S

E T

BARON ANGLAIS.

BARON BELGE (Ancien)

E U

E.DOUARD.

E V

E W

E X

BARON ALLEMAND.

BARON SUÉDOIS.

E Y

E Z

BARON FRANÇAIS.

F

F.G

F.H

F.I

F.L

F.K

PRINCE du SANG

MARQUIS

F.L

F.M

COMTE

ELISABETH

C^{nne} des ENFANTS de FRANCE
(puinés)

VIDAME

F.N

F.O

F.P

F.Q

F.R

F·S

F·T

F·U

F·V

F·W

F·X
—
C.ᴺᴺᴱ ᴅᴇ Lᴏᴜɪs Pʜɪʟɪᴘᴘᴇ 1ᴱᴿ

FRÉDÉRIC

F·Y
—
Cᴏᴜʀᴏɴɴᴇ·Rᴏʏᴀʟᴇ

F·Z

G

G·H

G·I

G·J

G · K

G · L

G · M

G · N

GASTON

C^{nne} DE MARQUIS
Ancienne

G · O

G · P

G · Q

G · R

G · S

C^{nne} MURALE, ANTIQUE

G · T

C^{nne} NAVALE ou ROSTRALE

G · U

C^{nne} MURALE

G · V

G · y

G · W

G · Z

G · X

H

H · I

C^{nne} Royale d'Angleterre

Georges
—

C^{nne} du Prince de Galles

H · j

H · K

H · L

H · M

H · N

H · O

H · P

H · Q

H · R

H · S

COUR · DES COUSINS ET NEVEUX ·

COUR · DES PETITS ENFANTS DE LA REINE ·

COUR · ANGLAISE DES ENFANTS DE LA REINE

✠ HYACINTHE · ✠

H · T

H · U

H · V

H · W

H · X

H·Y

I·J

H·Z

I·K

I

I·L

I·M

I·N

I·O

I·P

I·Q

I·T

I·R

I·S

I·V

I·U

I·W

I·X

I·Y

I·Z

J

J·K

J·L

COVR^{NNE} du CIMIER ANGLAIS.

JANE.

J·M

J·N

J·O

J·P

J·Q

J · R

J · S

Cᴺᴺᴱ ᴅᴇ Cᴏᴍᴛᴇ
Anglais.

J · T

J · U

J · V

J · W

LÉONIE.

J · X

J · Y

J · Z

K

K · L
Cᴺᴺᴱ Mᴜʀᴀʟᴇ ᴅᴇ ʟᴀ Vɪʟʟᴇ ᴅᴜ HAVRE.

K · M

K · N
Cᴺᴺᴱ Mᴜʀᴀʟᴇ ᴅᴇ ʟᴀ Vɪʟʟᴇ ᴅᴇ NÎMES.

C^{nne} ANTIQUE.

k·R

k·S

k·O

K·P

k·Q

C^{nne} MURALE de la Ville de PARIS.

C^{nne} M^{le} de la V. de VERSAILLES

LOUIS.

k·T

k·U

k·V

k·W

k·x

k·y

k·z

L

L · M

L · N

L · O

L · P

L · Q

L · R

L · S

L · T

TOQUES
DÉLECTEUR
ET PRINCE
2ᵉ EMPIRE
DU

Luxembourg

L · U

L · V

L · W

L · X

L · Y

L · Z

M · M

M · N

M · O

MATHILDE.

Cᵗᵉˢˢᵉ de Prince et Prince Souverain.
Cᵗᵉˢˢᵉ de Prince du Saint-Empire.

M · Q

M · P

M · R

M · S

Cᵗᵉˢˢᵉ des Archiducs ᵐ Q d'Autriche

M · T

M · U

M·V

M·W

M·X

M·y

M·Z

N·

N·O

N·P

N·Q

N·R

N—S

N·T

Cᵐ de COMTE —   — du Sᵗ EMPIRE·

Marguerite

—

Couronne des Grands-Ducs de Russie

N · U

N · W

N · Y

Nicolas

Cᵗᵉ des Ducs et Pairs D'Angleterre

Chapeau de Dignité

Cᵗᵉ des Marquis et Pairs D'Angl·

N · V

N · X

N · Z

O ·

O · P

O · Q

O · R

O · S

O · T

P · W

P · X

P · y

P · Z

vraíe Couronne
du Sacre
des anciens Rois
de POLOGNE.

Pierre

Bibliothèque de M.r le Comte de O

Q

Q · R

Q · S

Q · T

Roî de SIAM

Q · U

Q · V

Q · W

Q · Y

Q · X
COURONNE DE COMTE BELGE

Q · Z
CHEVALIER NOBLE NÉERLANDAIS.

R

R · S

R · T

COURONNE → dite → DE → CHARLEMAGNE

R · U

Robert. 1879

R · V

R · W

R · X

R . Y

R . Z

S

S . T

SOPHIE

SUZANNE

Coiffure des Doges, ou Ducs de Venise.

SÉBASTIEN

Couronne Rostrale — Rome Antique

Proposition de Couronne pour l'Empire Chinois.

Couronne de Fer des anciens Rois Lombards.

S . U

S . V

S . W

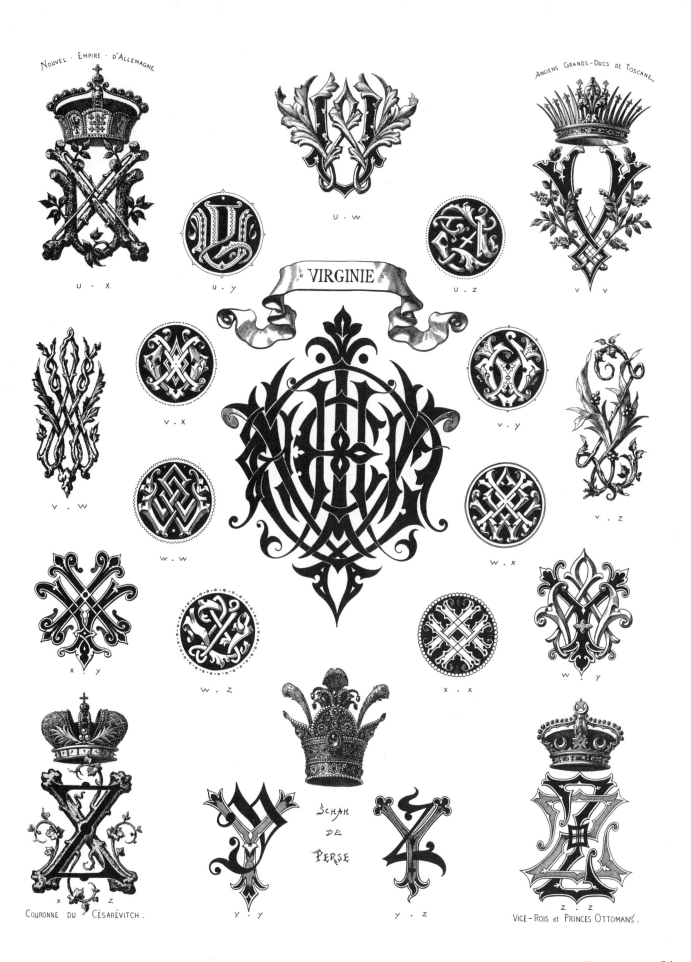

NOUVEL · EMPIRE · D'ALLEMAGNE

ANCIENS GRANDS-DUCS DE TOSCANE

u · w

VIRGINIE

u · x

u · y

u · z

v · v

v · x

v · y

v · w

w · w

w · x

v · z

x · y

w · z

x · x

w · y

COURONNE DU CÉSARÉVITCH.

SCHAH DE PERSE

x · z

y · y

y · z

z · z

VICE-ROIS et PRINCES OTTOMANS.

MONOGRAMMES · STYLES MOYEN AGE · ET RENAISSANCE
Composés et Gravés par Ch. DEMENGEOT.

Nᵒˢ 1. A.G   2. VICTOR   3. F.S   4. O. LARRI   5. ROSINE

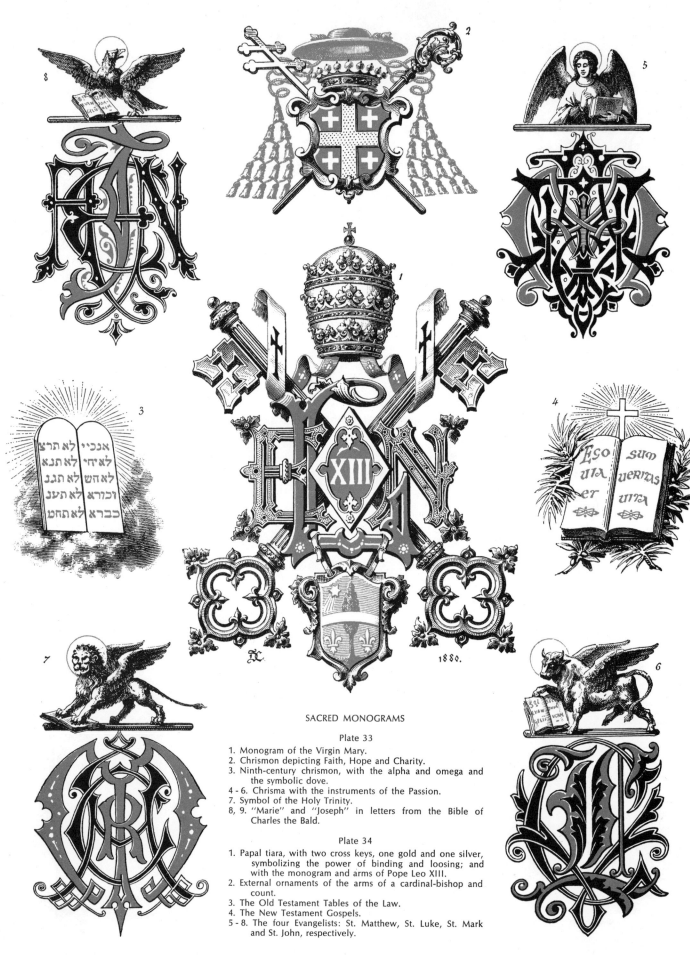

SACRED MONOGRAMS

Plate 33

1. Monogram of the Virgin Mary.
2. Chrismon depicting Faith, Hope and Charity.
3. Ninth-century chrismon, with the alpha and omega and the symbolic dove.
4 - 6. Chrisma with the instruments of the Passion.
7. Symbol of the Holy Trinity.
8, 9. "Marie" and "Joseph" in letters from the Bible of Charles the Bald.

Plate 34

1. Papal tiara, with two cross keys, one gold and one silver, symbolizing the power of binding and loosing; and with the monogram and arms of Pope Leo XIII.
2. External ornaments of the arms of a cardinal-bishop and count.
3. The Old Testament Tables of the Law.
4. The New Testament Gospels.
5 - 8. The four Evangelists: St. Matthew, St. Luke, St. Mark and St. John, respectively.

HERALDIC HELMETS

1. Helmet of emperors and kings
2. Dukes, princes and sovereign princes
3. Marquesses
4. Counts (earls) and viscounts
5. Barons

6. Knights
7. Gentlemen of three races
8. The newly ennobled
9. Bastards

Monograms and Ciphers

BY H. RENOIR

Monograms and Ciphers

DESIGNED BY

H. RENOIR, Heraldic Artist.

COMPLETE COLLECTION—ALPHABETICALLY ARRANGED.

LONDON AND EDINBURGH:
A. FULLARTON AND COMPANY.

A·A   A A   A A

A A   A B   A B

A B   A B   A B

A C   A C   A C

A D   A D   A D

A D   A E   A E

A E   A E   A F

A F   A F   A G

AG AG AH

AH AH AH

AH AI AI

AJ AJ AK

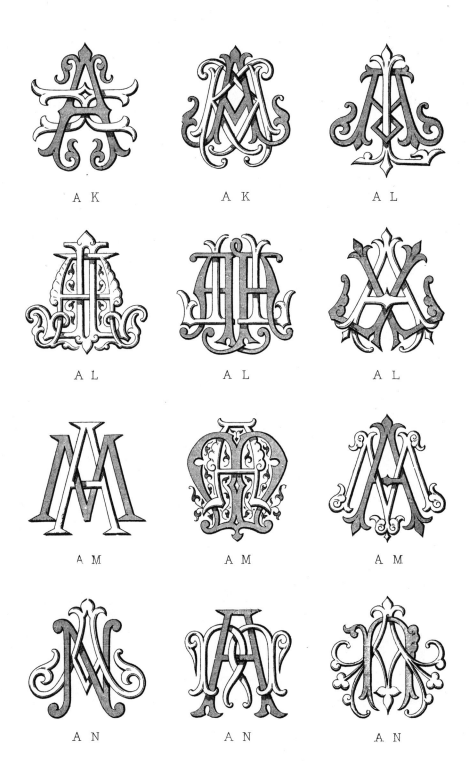

A K   A K   A L

A L   A L   A L

A M   A M   A M

A N   A N   A N

A O   A O   A P

A P   A P   A Q

A R   A R   A R

A S   A S   A S

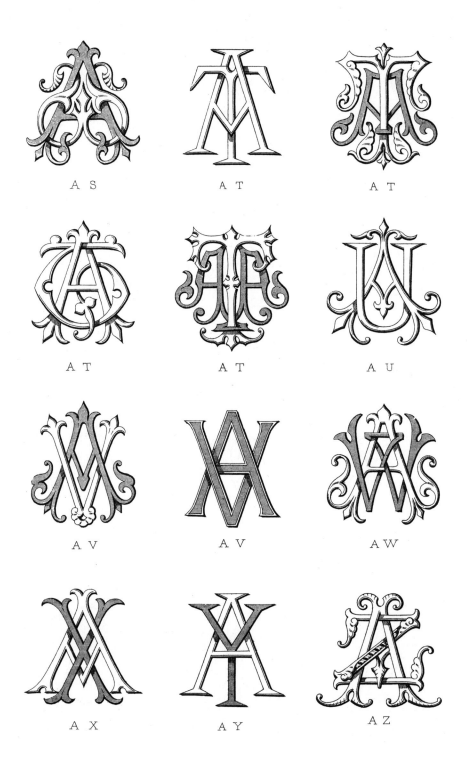

A S   A T   A T

A T   A T   A U

A V   A V   A W

A X   A Y   A Z

B B   B B   B B

B B   B C   B C

B C   B C   B D

B D   B D   B E

B E   B E   B F

B F   B G   B G

B G   B G   B G

B H   B H   B H

B H   B H   B I

B I   B J   B J

B J   B K   B K

B L   B L   B L

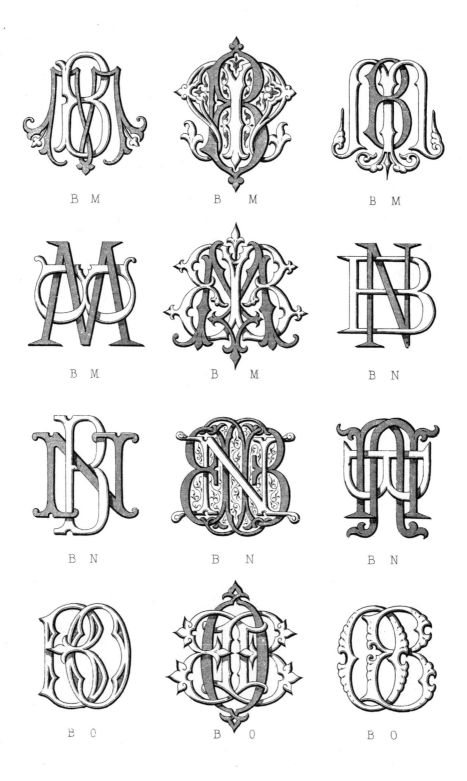

B M   B M   B M

B M   B M   B N

B N   B N   B N

B O   B O   B O

B P B P B P

B P B Q B Q

B R B R B R

B S B S B S

B T   B T   B T

B U   B V   B V

B V   B W   B W

B X   B Y   B Z

C C   C C   C C C

C C   C D   C D

C   C D   C D

C D   C E   C E

C E   C E   C F

C F   C F   C G

C G   C G   C H

C H   C H   C I

C I   C J   C J

C K   C K   C L

C L   C L   C L

C M   C M   C M

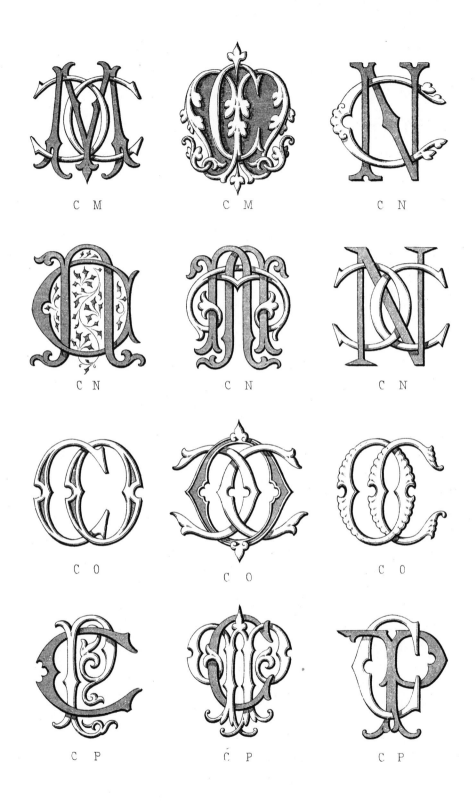

C M   C M   C N

C N   C N   C N

C O   C O   C O

C P   C P   C P

C P   C P   C Q

C Q   C R   C R

C R   C R   C S

C S   C S   C S

C T   C T   C T

C U   C V   C V

C V   C W   C W

C X   C Y   C Z

D D   D D   D D

D E   D E   D E

D E   D F   D F

D G   D G   D G

D G   D G   D G

D H   D H   D H

D H   D H   D I

D I   D J   D J

D J   D J   D K

D K   D L   D L

D L   D M   D M

D M   D M   D M

D N   D N   D N

D O   D O   D O

D P   D P   D P

D Q   D Q   D R

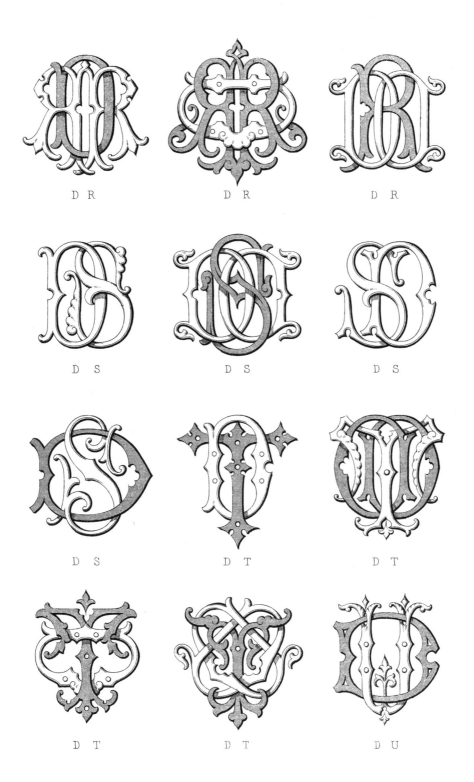

D R   D R   D R

D S   D S   D S

D S   D T   D T

D T   D T   D U

D V   D V   D V

D W   D W   D W

D X   D Y   D Z

E E   E E   E E

E F   E F   E F

E G   E G   E G

E G   E H   E H

E H   E H   E I

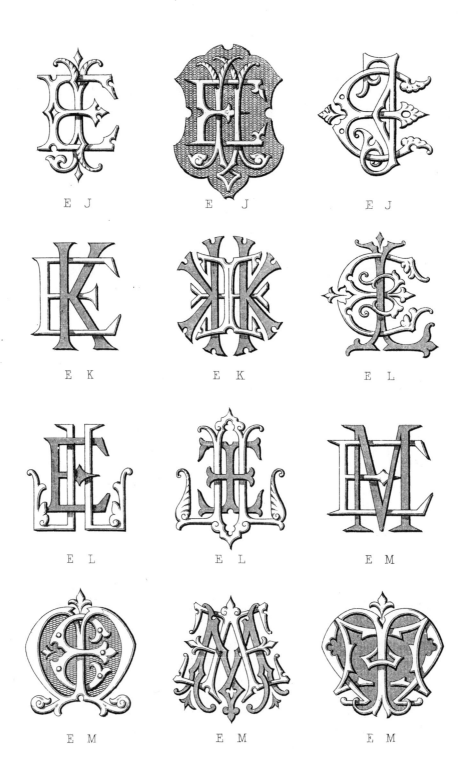

E J E J E J

E K E K E L

E L E L E M

E M E M E M

E N   E N   E N

E O   E O   E O

E P   E P   E P

E Q   E R   E R

E R E S E S

E S E T E T

E T E T E U

E V E V E V

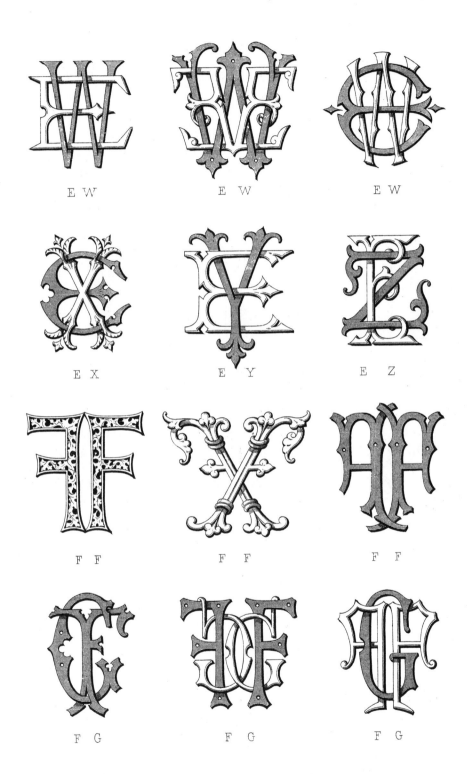

E W   E W   E W

E X   E Y   E Z

F F   F F   F F

F G   F G   F G

F H   F H   F H

F I   F I   F J

F J   F K   F L

F L   F L   F L

F M   F M   F M

F M   F N   F N

F N   F O   F O

F P   F P   F P

F Q   F Q   F R

F R   F S   F S

F S   F.T   F T

F T   F U   F U

F V   F V   F W

F W   F X   F Y

F Y   F Z   F Z

G G   G G   G G

GH GH GH

GI GI GJ

GJ GJ GK

GK GL GL

G M   G M   G M

G N   G N   G N

G O   G O   G O

G P   G P   G P

G Q   G R   G R

G R   G S   G S

G T   G T   G U

G V   G V   G V

G W　　　　G W　　　　G X

G Y　　　　G Y　　　　G Z

H H　　　　H H　　　　H H

H I　　　　H J　　　　H J

H K   H K   H L

H L   H L   H M

H M   H M   H N

H N   H O   H O

H P   H P   H P

H Q   H R   H R

H S   H S   H S

H T   H T   H U

H V   H V   H W

H X   H Y   H Z

I I   I J   I J

I J   I K   I L

I L   I M   I N

I N   I O   I P

I P   I Q   I Q

I R   I R   I S

I T   I T   I U

I V   I V   I W

! X   I Y   I Z

J J   J J   J J

JK   JK   JL

JL   JL   JM

JM   JM   JN

JO   JO   JP

J P   J P   J . Q

J R   J R   · J S

J S   J T   J T

J T   J U   J V

J V   J W   J W

J X   J Y   J Z

K K   K K   K L

K L   K L   K M

K M   K M   K M.

K N   K N   K O

K O   K P   K P

K Q   K R   K R

K S

K S

K T

K T

K U

K V

K V

K W

K X

K X

K Y

K Z

L L   L L   L M

L M   L M   L N

L N   L O   L O

L O   L P   L P

L P   L P   L Q

L R   L R   L R

L S   L S   L T

L T   L U   L V

L V   L W   L W

L X   L Y   L Z

M M   M M   M M

M N   M N   M O

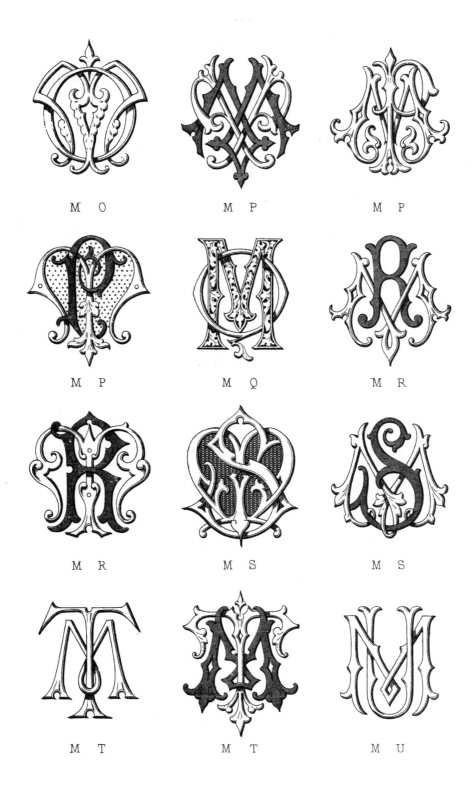

M O   M P   M P

M P   M Q   M R

M R   M S   M S

M T   M T   M U

M V   M V   M W

M X   M Y   M Z

N N   N N   N O

N P   N P   N P

N Q   N R   N R

N S   N S   N S

N T   N T   N U

N V   N V   N W

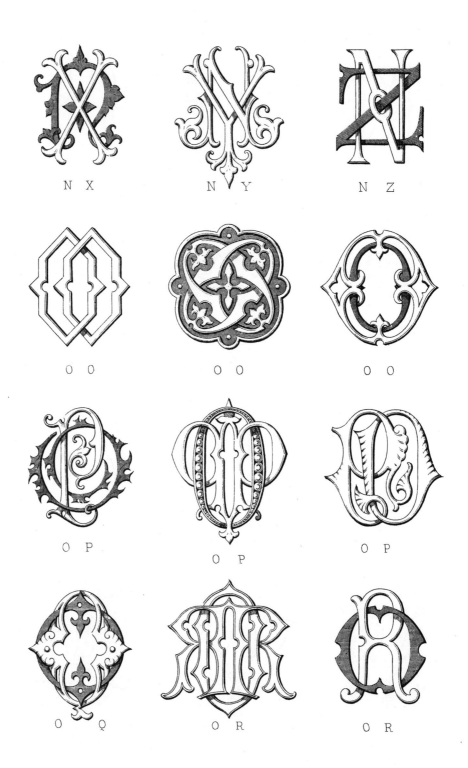

N X   N Y   N Z

O O   O O   O O

O P   O P   O P

O Q   O R   O R

O S   O S   O T

O U   O V   O V

O W   O X   O Y

O Z   P P   P P

P Q   P R   P R

P S   P S   P S

P T   P T   P T

P U   P U   P V

P V   P W   P W

P X   P X   P Y

P Z   Q Q   Q R

Q S   Q T   Q U

Q V   Q V   Q W

Q X   Q Y   Q Z

R R   R R   R R

R S   R S   R S

R T   R T   R U

R V   R V   R W

R X   R Y   R Z

S S   S S   S S

S T   S T   S U

S V   S V   S W

S X   S Y   S Z

T T   T T   T T

T U   T V   T V

T W   T X   T Y

T Z   U U   U V

U W   U X   U Y

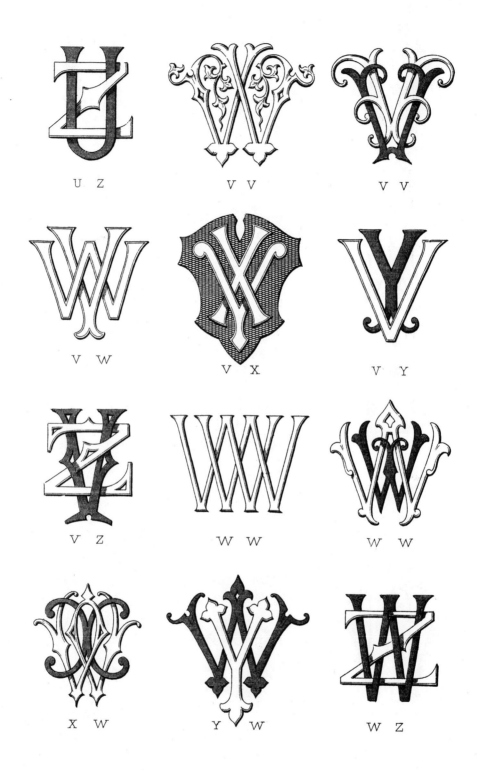

U Z   V V   V V

V W   V X   V Y

V Z   W W   W W

X W   Y W   W Z

X X   X Y   X Z

Y Y   Y Z   Z Z

G E   M M   S B

A A   H H   O M

MATHILDE   EUGÉNIE   CLOTILDE

MARIE   VICTORIA   MARIA

MARTHE   JEANNE   CLAIRE

THÉRÉSA   AMÉLIE   HÉLÈNE

S D   H H   M A

H B J   H R   A C B

M M   A B   B A

M R   C S   A E L

IHS

IHS

IHS

A M

INRI

A M

SEMPER

I M

RECUERDO

AEI

AEI

AEI

New Book of Seven Hundred & Fifty Eight
Plain, Ornamented & Reversed Cyphers

BY F. KNIGHT

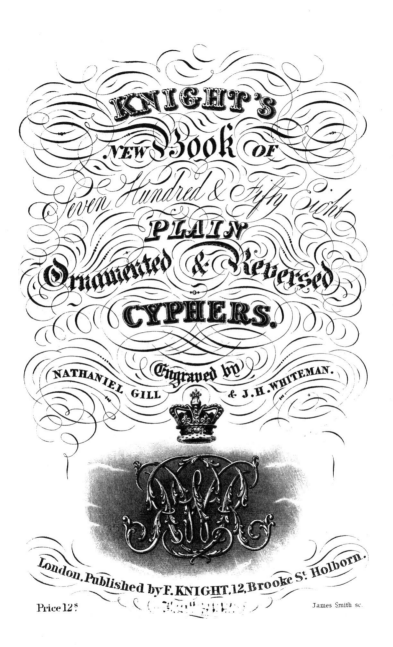

KNIGHT'S NEW Book OF Seven Hundred & Fifty Eight PLAIN Ornamented & Reversed CYPHERS.

Engraved by

NATHANIEL GILL & J.H. WHITEMAN.

London, Published by F. KNIGHT, 12, Brooke S.t Holborn.

Price 12.s

James Smith sc.

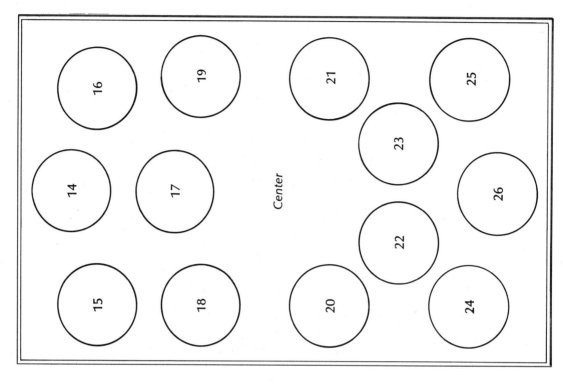

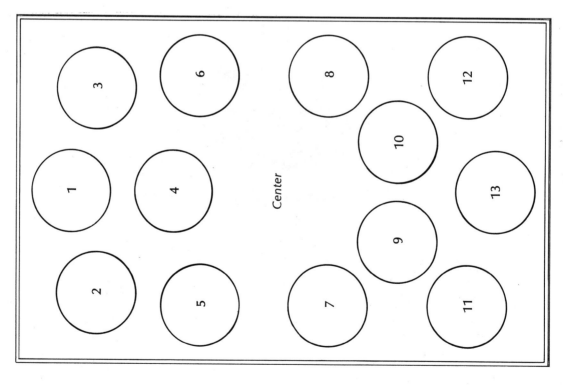

These diagrams show the sequence of monograms in 'Knight's New Book'

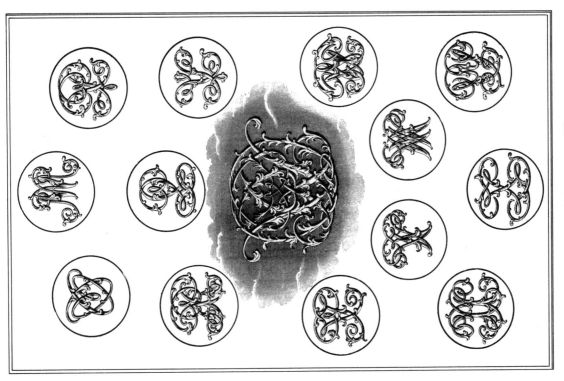

NN – ZZ; center: GD

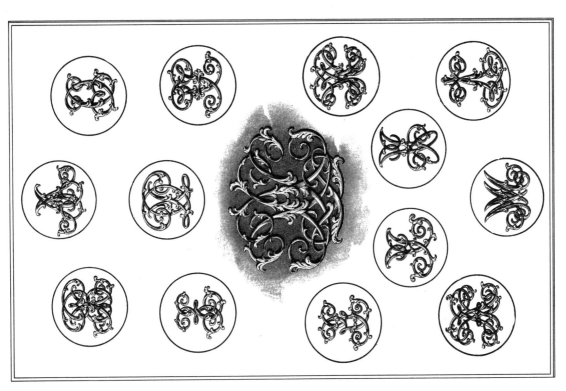

AA – MM; center: SL

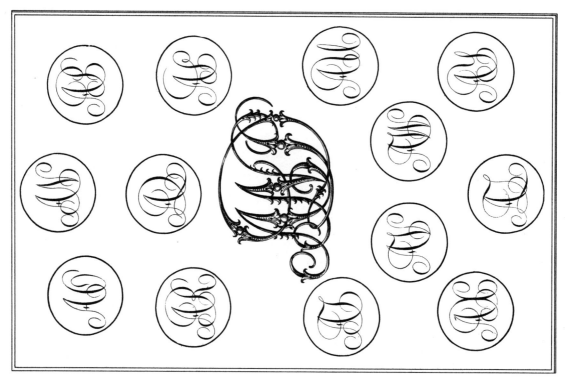

AN – AZ; center: AND

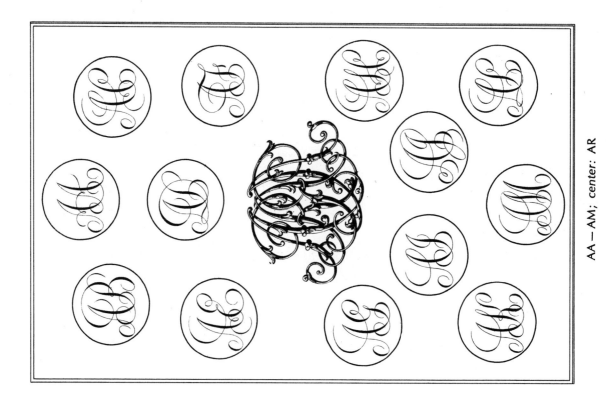

AA – AM; center: AR

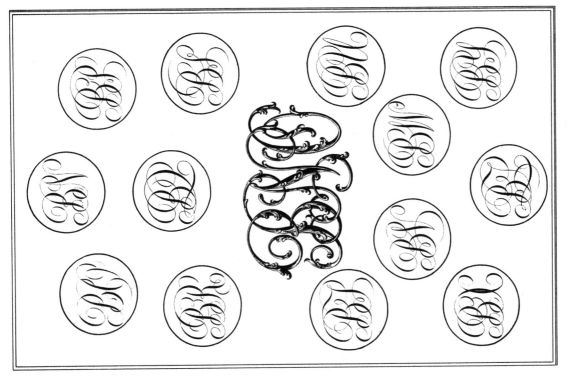

BN — BZ; center: BNO

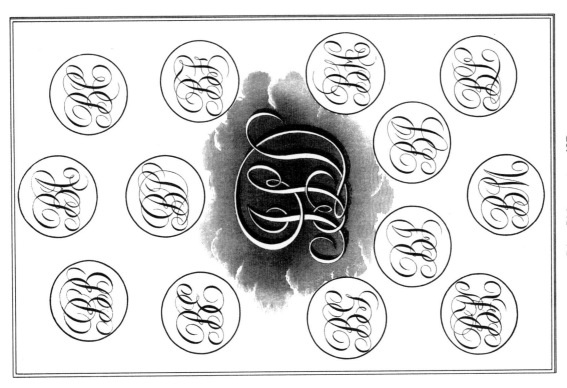

BA — BM; center: ISD

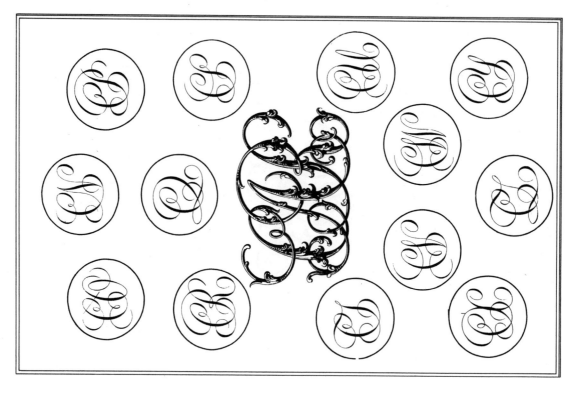

CN — CZ; center: CAR

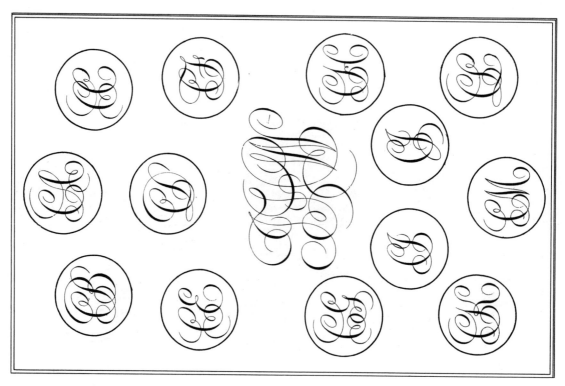

CA — CM; center: IHW

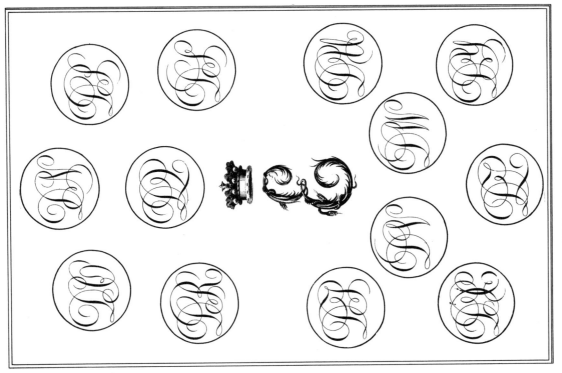

DN — DZ; center: E

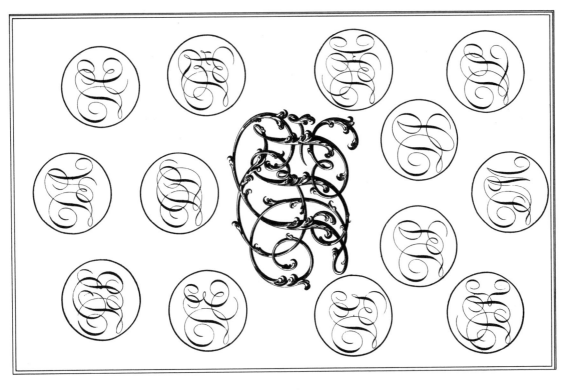

DA — DM; center: DSF

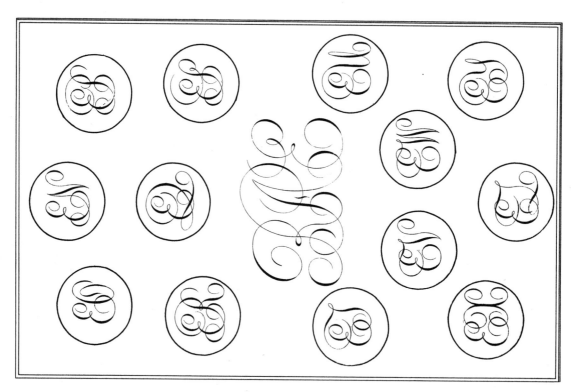

EN — EZ; center: RAE

EA — EM; center: EL

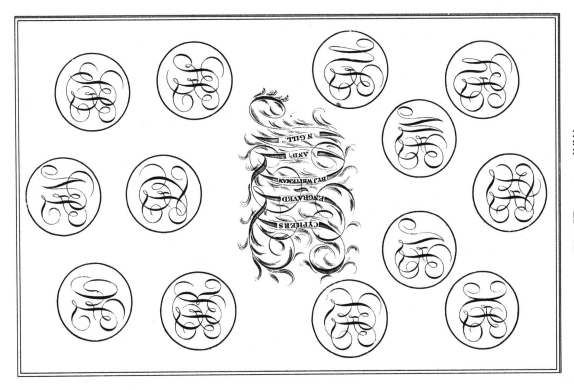

FN — FZ; center: IHW

FA — FM; center: GB

GA — GM; center: CC

GN — GZ; center: GIR

HN — HZ; center: HIB

HA — HM; center: CB

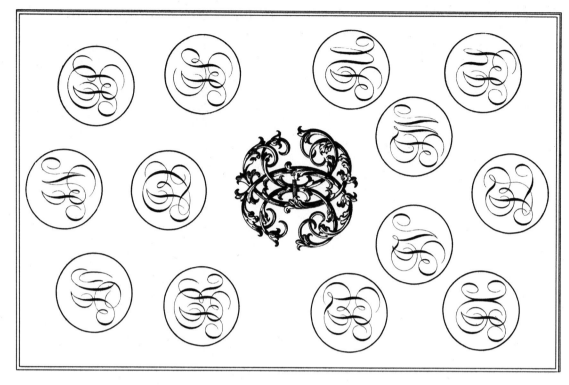

IN – IZ; center: CX

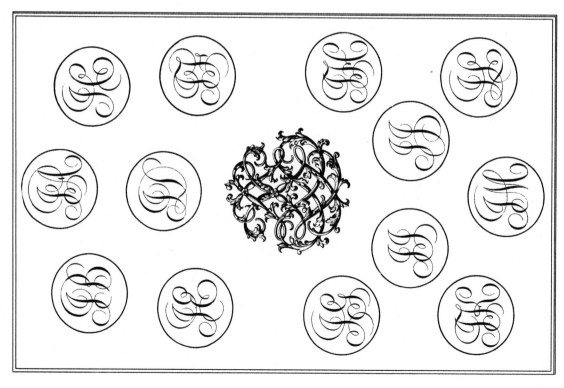

IA – IM; center: LL

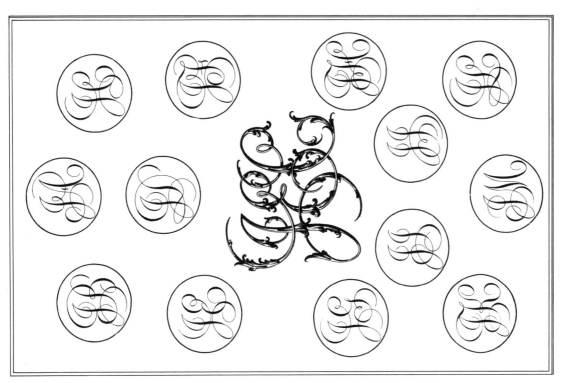

JN — JZ; center: JLB

JA — JM; center: JEC

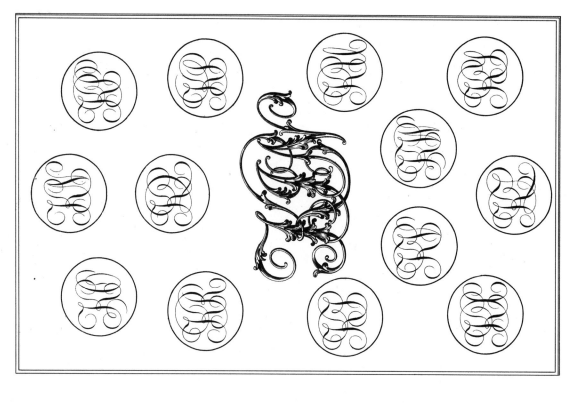

KN – KZ; center: KIN

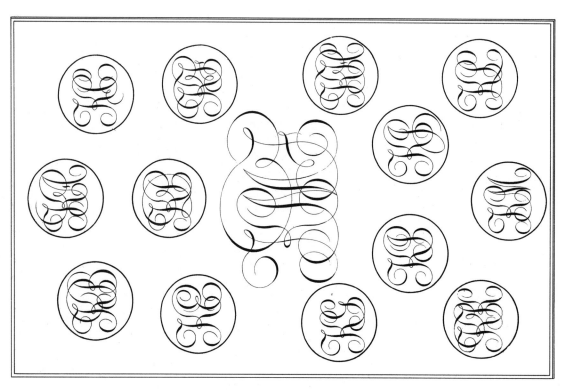

KA – KM; center: KMF

LN — LZ; center: BCP

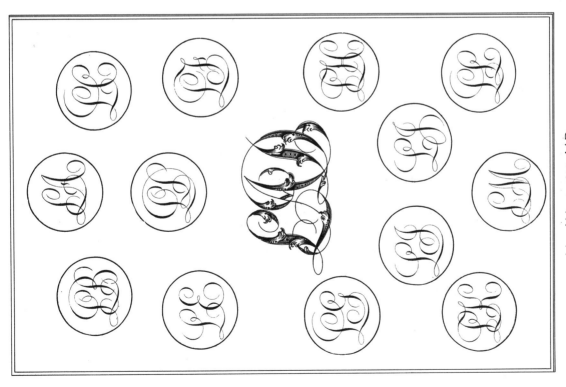

LA — LM; center: LAD

Knight • **123**

MA — MM; center: MEN

MN — MZ; center: RR

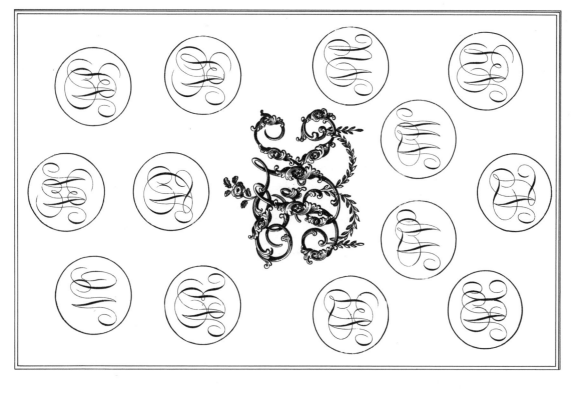

NN–NZ; center: FK

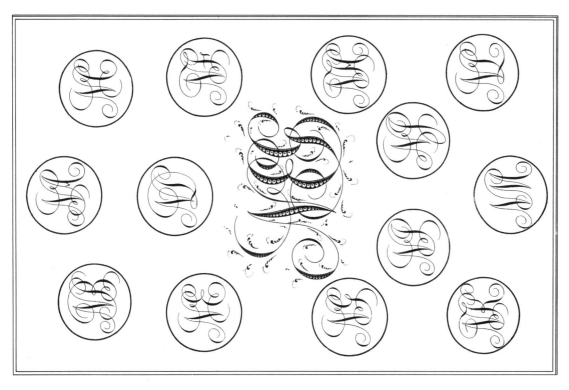

NA–NM; center: NEG

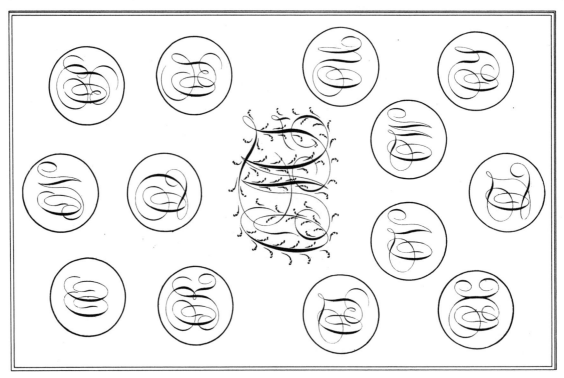

ON – OZ; center: OMF

OA – OM; center: EW

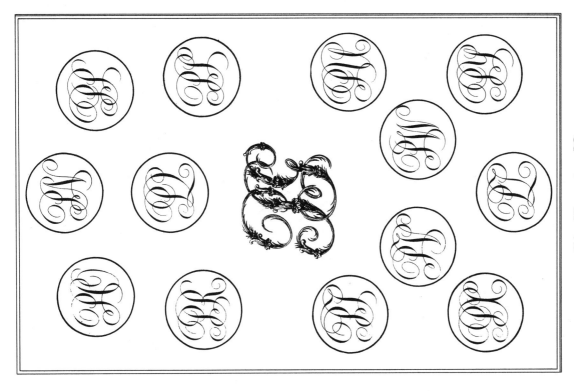

PN — PZ; center: PG

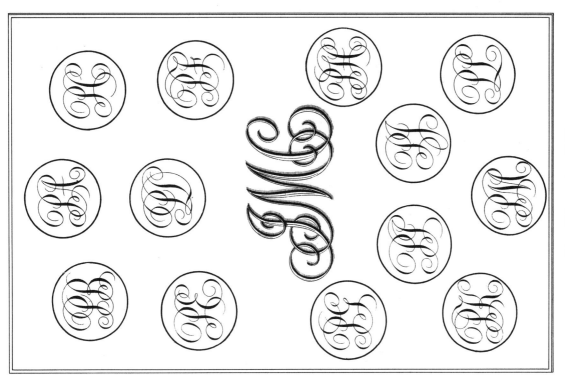

PA — PM; center: IMC

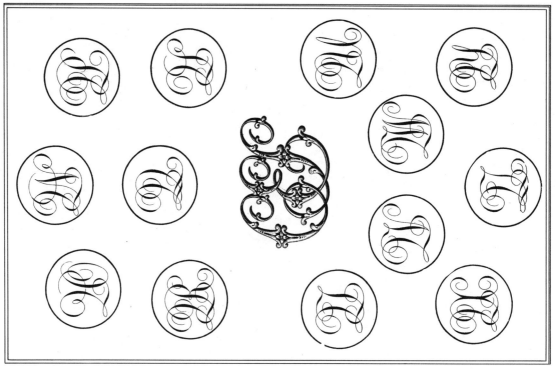

QN – QZ; center: CES

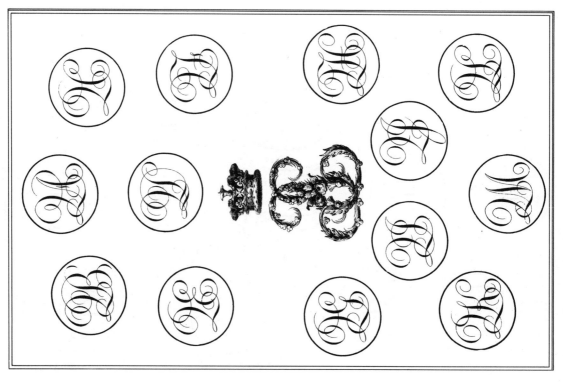

QA – QM; center: EE

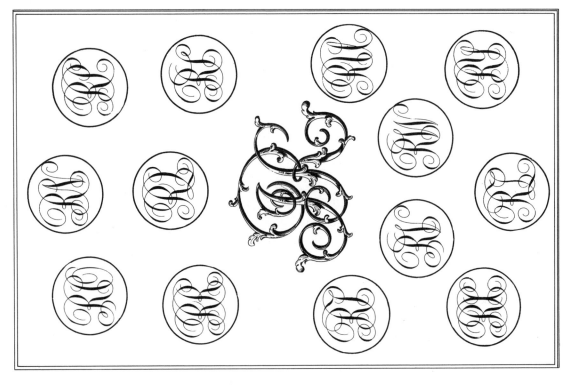

RN – RZ; center: IR

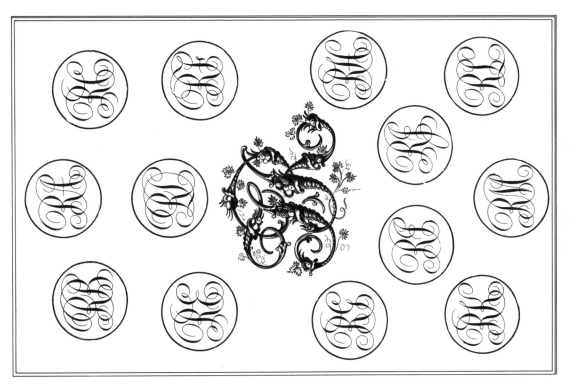

RA – RM; center: TR

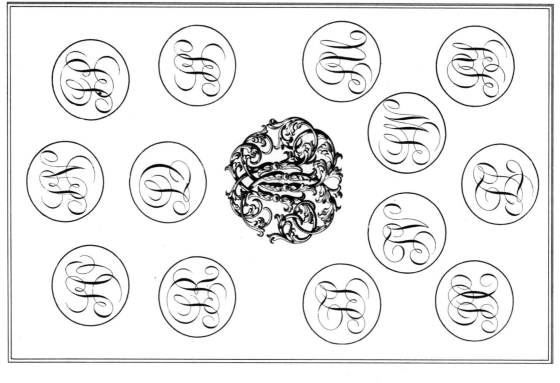

SN — SZ; center: SC

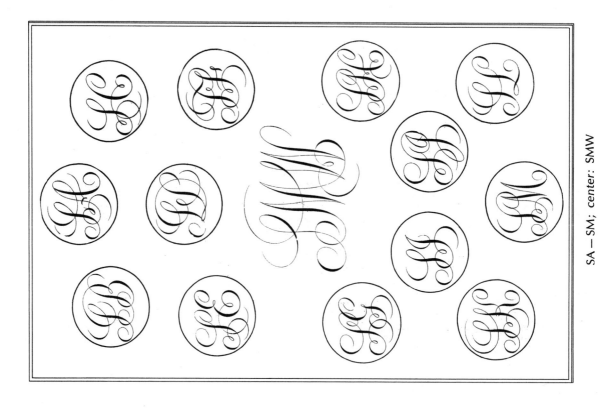

SA — SM; center: SMW

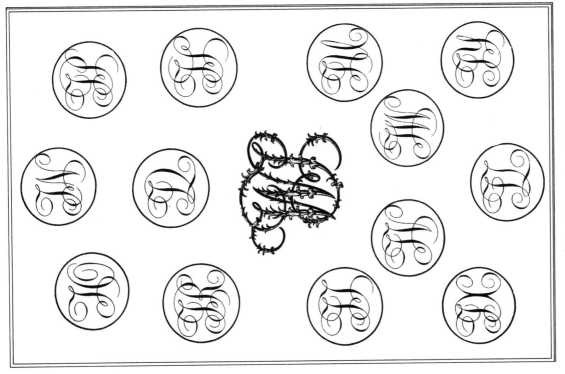

TN — TZ; center: WT

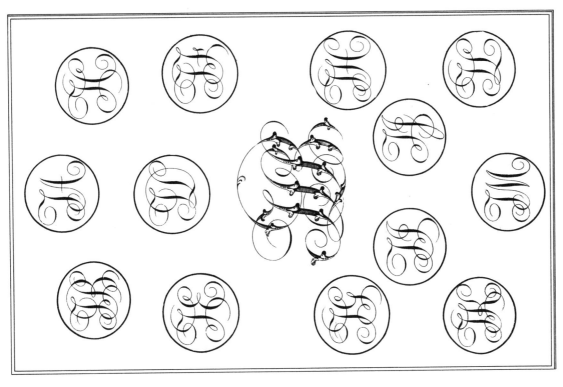

TA — TM; center: TLB

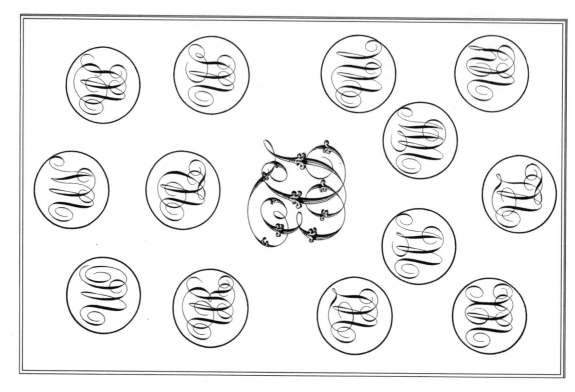

UN – UZ; *center:* ECT

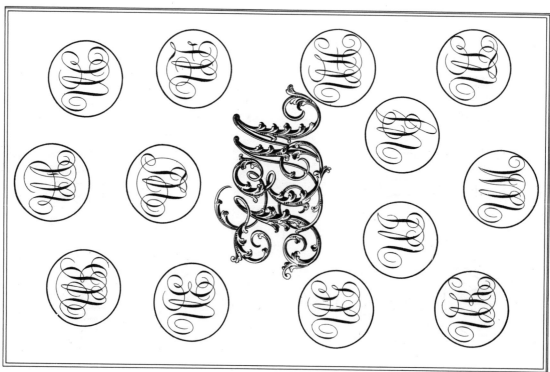

UA – UM; *center:* TEM

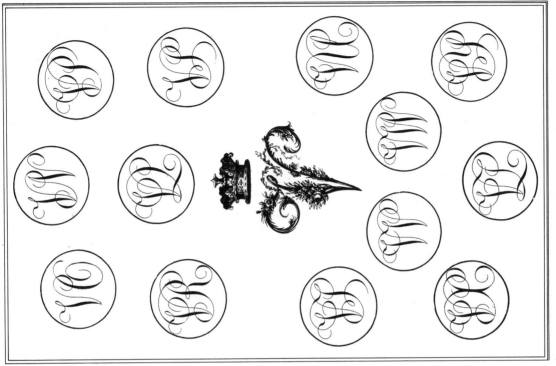

VN – VZ; center: V

VA – VM; center: VAD

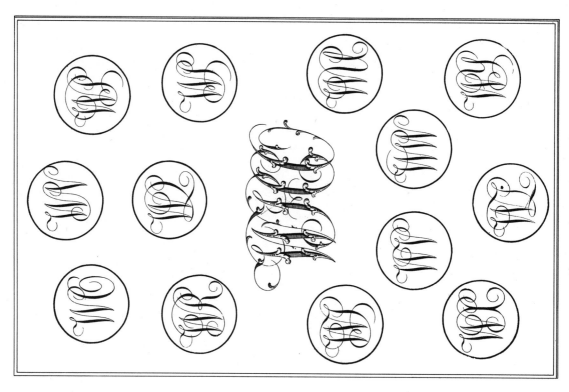

WN — WZ; center: WHO

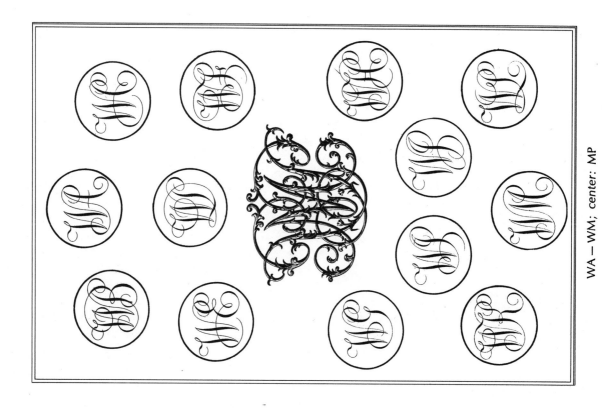

WA — WM; center: MP

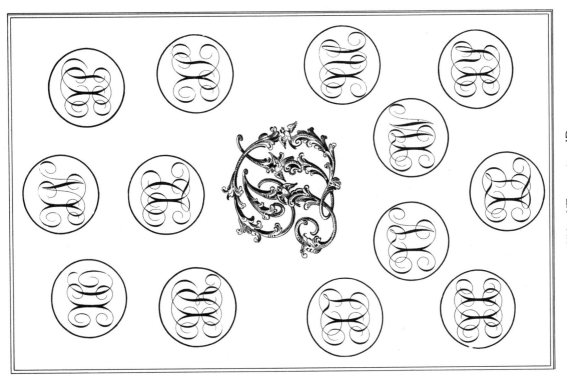

XN — XZ; center: ID

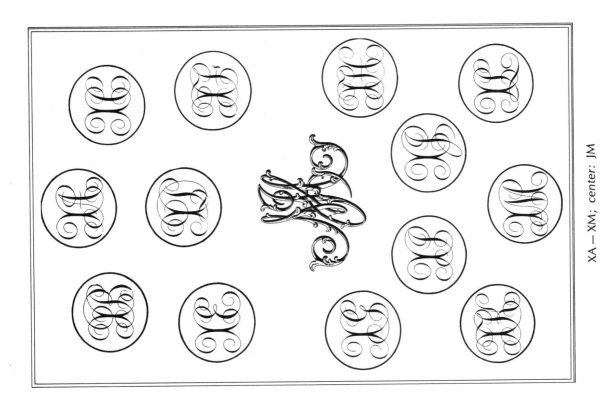

XA — XM; center: JM

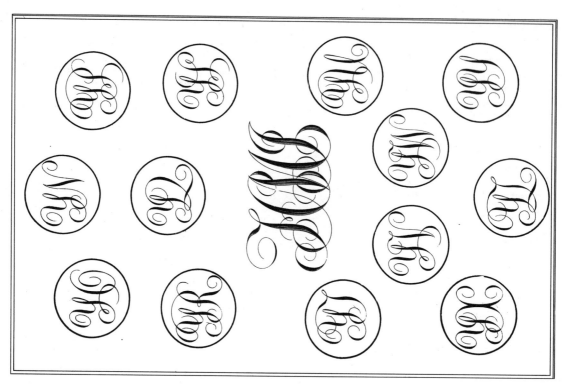

YN — YZ; center: HMI

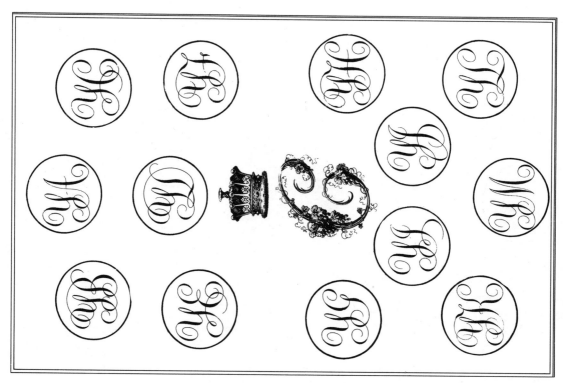

YA — YM; center: C

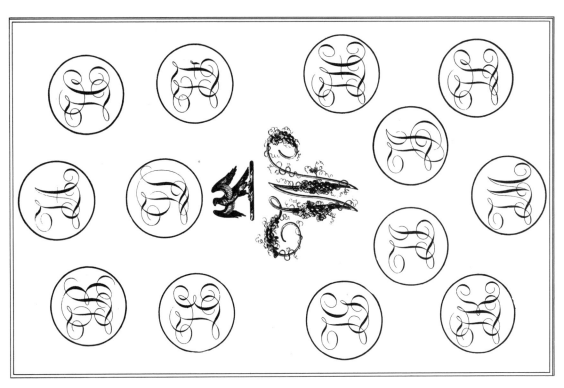

ZN – ZZ; center: AL

ZA – ZM; center: W

Monograms in Three and Four Letters

BY J. GORDON SMITH

MONOGRAMS

IN

THREE AND FOUR LETTERS

SUITABLE FOR

Engraving, Painting, Piercing, Embroidering, Carving, &c.

DESIGNED BY

J. GORDON SMITH,

HERALDIC ARTIST.

New Series.

LONDON:

THOMAS C. JACK, 45 LUDGATE HILL.

EDINBURGH: GRANGE PUBLISHING WORKS.

J . H . A .

M . E . A .

G . J . A .

E . N . A .

T . L . A .

M . C . A .

A . A . S . A .

A G N E S .

E . T . A .

W . O . A .

A . E . A .

T . S . A .

W . J . A .

J. O. A.

S. L. A.

C. B. E. A.

J. M. W. A.

"ALICE"

V. G. A.

A. A. A.

M. B. A.

E. H. A.

S.ᵀ A.

T.H.A.

R.A & Cᵒ

W.E.A.

S.G.A.

C.J.A.

O.G.F.A.

N.E.S.A.

T.B.A.

V.M.A.

G.C.A.

P.C.A.

G.T.O.A.

ANNIE

W.F.A.

J.A.A.

G.K.F.A.

D.F.A.

J . T . B .

W . E . B .

M . A . B .

N . O . C . B .

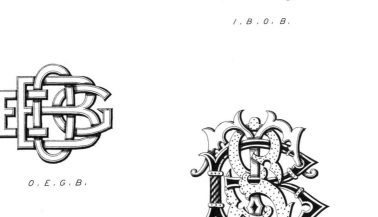

I . B . O . B .

G . F . B .

O . E . G . B .

T . S . B .

B . B . 1880 .

B E T S Y.

O . B . B .

B E L L A .

J . M . B .

O . S . B .

C . D . B .

A . D . B .

N . H . M . B .

H . C . B .

E . C . B .

C . K . B .

T . M . Mc B .

W . H . B .

FRANCES H.B.

C . S . B .

N . G . B .

B . C . B .

C . A . B .

I . B . B .

L . E . B .

K . S . B .

P . J . B .

G and B .

M . L . B .

S . G . B .

C . W . B .

J . A . C . B .

J . E . C .

V . O . C .

L . E . C .

E . T . C .

S.t A . B . C .

M.c C .

Charlie C .

M . A . D . C .

S . B . G . C .

J . A . S . C .

CELIA.

B E . C .

D . Mᶜ C .

A . C . C .

P . D . C .

D . L . T . C .

ST E . C . C .
1881.

B . G . C .

T . C . C .

M & C .

D . E . C .

E . C . C .

H . C & C?

W . G . A . C .

P . E . C .

L . R . B . C .

N . S . C .

E. G. C.

M. G. C.

H. M. C.

I. D. C.

CARRIE.

C. E. C.

S. P. C.

CLAUD.

E. D. B. C.

M . A . D .

A & M . D .

F . E . D .

B . C . D . D .

B E N J A M I N D .

L . G . D .

M . B . D .

W . S . D .

A . J . D .

C . H . D .

C . E . D .

S . S . D .

A . C . D .

D A V I D

M . E . S . D .

E . C . M♀ D .

D O R A .

T . E . D .

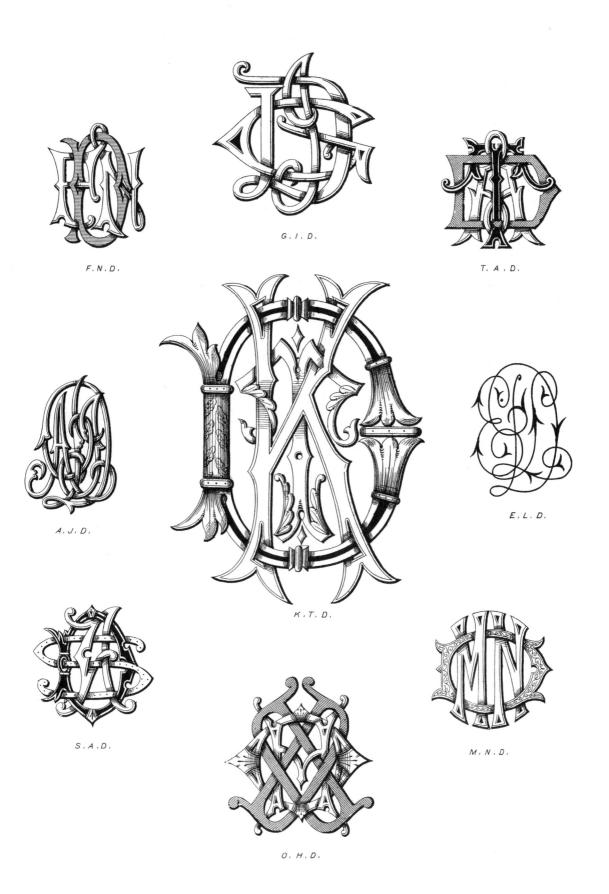

F.N.D.

G.I.D.

T.A.D.

A.J.D.

K.T.D.

E.L.D.

S.A.D.

O.H.D.

M.N.D.

J . U . E .

E . C . E .

M . A . E .

D . S . Mc E .

S . C . E .

A . K . E .

A . Mc E .

C . P . C . E .

M . T . E .

W.S.E.

M.V.E.

T.R.E.

G.H.E.

J.B.E.

I.H.E.

B.C.E.

ELIZA.

E.J.E.

D.B.E.

EDITH.

D.C.E.

I.E.E.

EMILY.

K.H.McE.

H.W.E.

EVALINE.

G.I.E.

C. A. F.

A. H. F.

H. N. F.

M. L. F.

W. S. F.

G. R. F.

M. F. M. F.

J. G. F.

L. N. F.

T. C. F.

J. B. F.

M . R . F .

T . G . F .

E . L . F .

C . H . F .

FANNY.

J . G . F .

J . H . M . F .

B . D . F .

G . C . F .

L . A . F .

G . J . F .

S . G . F .

R . Mᶜ F .

FLORA .

O . G . F .

E . H . F .

D . S . O . F .

B . F & Cᵒ

B. E. G.

E. D. G.

ST G.

W. A. G.

GEORGE.

F. A. G.

W. T. G.

L. K. N. G.

J. F. D. G.

C. E. G.

GERALD.

F. T. G.

M. E. G.

GERTIE.

K. T. G.

P. L. G.

E. S. G.

S. A. G.

O . C . G .

A . N . G

J . D . O . G .

A . T . G .

J . H . L . G .

T . L . G .

S . D . G .

J . C . S . G .

J . J . G .

B.N.H.

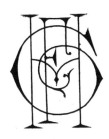

G.F.H.

E.G.H.

S.A.H.

C.A.H.H.

T & A.H.

H.A.H.

D.D.F.H.

T.E.H.

Smith · **167**

E.D.H.

Y.G.H.

G.L.N.H.

H.N.H.

HARRY

·E.I.H.

R.A & J.H.

J.P.H.

J.N.E.H.

F.M.H.

A.T.H.

N.E.D.H.

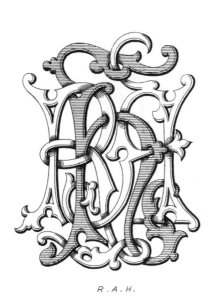

HANNAH,

R.A.H.

HATTIE

T.J.H.

HELEN G.

J.W.H.

M. C. I.

T. S. I.

H. L. I.

B. E. B. I.

K. T. I.

ISAAC.

C. E. D. I.

G. G. I.

W. P. I.

S.B.,S.I.

S.C.I.

B.G.I.

M.E.I.

E.G.I.

I.S.A.

C.G.J.I.

C.B.I.

H.D.G.I.

I . A . J .

E . L . J .

T . G . J .

JAMES S.

JANET.

T . C . J .

S . G . J .

A . D . J .

JANET.

W. J & C?

D. E. J

H. M. J.

JOE

JOHN.

JULIA.

JACK.

E. F. J.

JESSIE

A.G.K.

A.R.K.

T.C.K.

O. la K.

I.S.K.

KATE.

J.B.C.K.

O.N.H.K.

T.J.McK.

D.G.K.

J.A.K.

T. G. K.

E. T. K.

M. A. K.

I. G. K.

KATHERINE.

A. O. K.

J. R. K.

D. E. K.

C. H. K.

G.C.L.

S.E.L.

A.H.L.

J.A.L.

P.G.L.

LOUISA.

A.L.

LEWIS.

S.M.L.

A.B.L.

W.E.B.G.L.

G.A.L.

J.McL.

K.M.L.

LILY

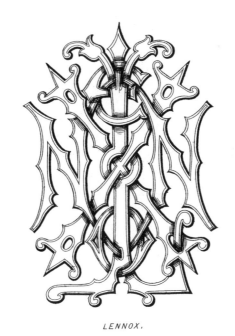

LENNOX.

LOUI

A.F.L.

M.L & Cº

E.J.L.

T.D.L.

G.H.F.L.

E.H.L.

F.D.L.

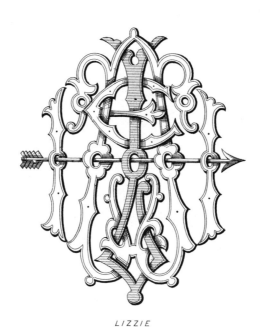

LIZZIE

M.C.L.

LOTTIE.

U.C.L.

B.C.L.

H.F.L.

V.M.L.

T.M.L.

J.E.L.

S & L.

H.S.L.

LUCY.

M.A.M.L.

T.S.L.

A. T. M.

H. E. N. M.

C. A. M.

G. S. M.

MARY.

A. Y. M.

A. G. H. M.

W. T. M.

P. H. M.

J . G . M .

R . S . M .

I . M . H . M .

A . H . M .

M . A . M .

I . A . M .

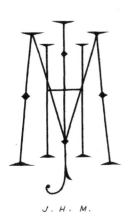

J . H . M .

G . A . M .

C . R . M .

J.S.M.

H.F.M.

W.W.M.

A.J.M.

A.V.M.

MAY

F.L.M.

C.K.Y.M.

D.M.M.

W.J.M.

G.A.M.

D.G.M.

N.H.M.

E & G.M.

E.C.M.

R.C.M.

MAUD.

B.O.M.

P.G.H.N.

H.G.N.

M.E.N.

T.E.N.

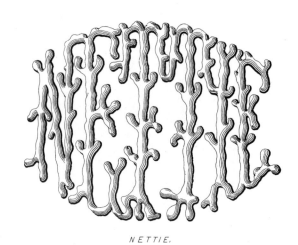

NETTIE.

W.I.N.

T.O.N.

S.B.N.

D.T.N.

G. H. N.

R. G. N.

S. I. N.

T. R. N.

J. S. N.

A. G. N.

T. A. N.

M. I. N.

G. Y. N.

NORA.

S^t N.

E.C.N.

T.H.N.

NELLY.

E.N.N.

E.B.N.

A.M.N.

J.E.N.

S.G.O.

J.E.D.O.

J.E.N.O.

I.M.O

OSWALD.

L.E.R.O.

M.W.A.O.

OLIVER.

F.E.O.

J.F.F.O.

A.S.O.

O.M.O.

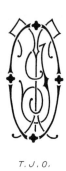

T.J.O.

F.G.O.

T.E.O.

I.G.O.O.

C.E.O.

H.D.O.

G.E.P.

H.T.P.

W.A.P.

B.F.P.

IN
MEMORY
OF

PETER.

J.A.P.

G.E.P.

J.G.P.

M.E.P.

J.W.P.

L.H.A.P.

O.M.P.

I.A.E.P.

A.G.P.

E.L.P.

G.S.P.

A.M.P.

W.M.P.

S.A.P.

W.G.P.

S.T.P.

PAUL.

JANE P.

PEARL.

H.B.P.

S.C.P.

G.H.P.

A . S . Q .

R . Mᶜ Q .

E . F . Q .

DON Q .

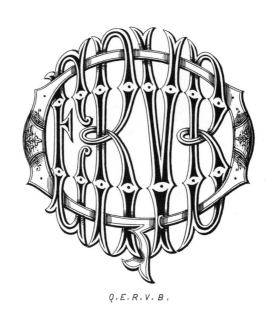

Q . E . R . V . B .

B de Q

N . M . E . Q .

J . S . Q .

R . E . H . Q .

J.E.R.

B.S.R.

T.S.R.

J & R.

ROSA.

E.S.R.

J.G.R.

M.C.M.R.

M.A.R.

T. U. H. R.

B. G. R.

CORA R.

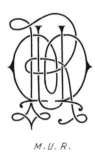

M. U. R.

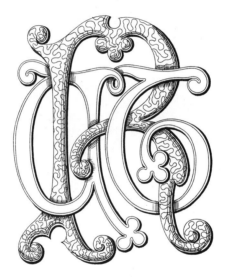

C. T. R.

I. G. R.

U. O. U. R.

O. S. R.

T. T. R.

G.H.R.

G.A.C.R.

J.E.R.

A.G.R.

M.S.R.

RALPH

G.L.H.R.

C.J.C.R.

A.H.R.

W . B . S .

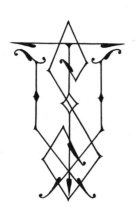

F . J . S .

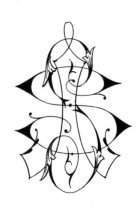

O . S . O . S .

T . U . S .

I . H . S .

A . S . S .

B . J . S .

G . G . S .

S U S A N .

B.R.S.

J.E.J.S.

H.C.S.

J.E.L.S.

J SMITH

C.G.S.

A.W.S.

P.A.S.

J.C.S.

A.R.S.

M & S.

C. K. S.

SARAH.

R. C. S.

A. A. S.

W. E. S.

A. O. S.

I. O. S.

E. M. B. S.

J. O. S.

W.A.S.

H.O.S.

A.E.S.

I.R.S.

STEPHEN.

I.S.S.

G.M.S.

J.T.S.

T.F.S.

C. M. T.

C. C. C. T.

K. C. T.

J. C. J. T.

M. M. T.

E. T. T.

H. A. T.

C. F. T.

A. D. G. T.

J. P. T.

TIMOTHY.

M & T.

O. S. G. T.

THERESA.

H & T.

A. F. T.

S. Mc T.

Y. A. T.

G. M. T.

G. C. T.

S. B. T.

E. S. T.

THOMAS.

S. G. T.

A. P. T.

W. M. S. T.

H. S. T.

B.O.E.T.

T.A.T.

D.H.T.

TOM.

G.F.T.

R.V.T.

L.U.T.

M.O.N.T.

A.S.T.

N. A. U

H. G. U

B. F. U.

G. S. U.

A. E. O. U.

E. I. U.

W. I. U.

T. S. U.

A. T. U.

A.L.V.

G.J.L.V.

M.A.V.

A.P.V.

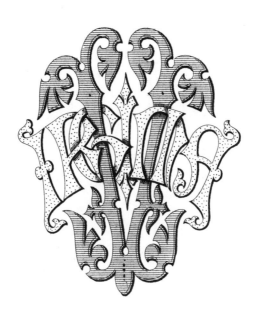

VIRGINIA.

J.C.V.

J.B.V.

VIVIAN.

VERNON.

A. G. W.

S. C. W.

C. E. W.

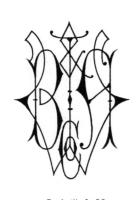

B. A. W & C?

A. V. F. W.

J. G. W.

M. C. W.

G. C. P. W.

E. R. W.

T.F.A.W.

G.A.A.W.

M.D.W.

I.E.V.W.

WINNIE.

F.G.D.W.

W.H.W.

A.O.W.

T.E.S.W.

J.T.W.

A.O.W.

E.T.S.W.

WILLIE.

A.N.W.

S.C.O.W.

R.D.W.

J.E.W.

S.C.W.

P. H. W.

J. C. W.

T. V. W.

A & R. W.

E. K. W.

W. A. W.

F. N. H. W.

T. Y. W.

L. M. W.

G.R.C.Y.

N.F.Y.

G.A.Y.

A.G.Y.

W.N.Y.

MARY Y.

J.G.Y.

A.M.M.Y.

A.B.Y.

A.M.Y.

A.G.Y.

A.J.Y.

A.S.Y.

S.Y & Cº

J.O.Y.

H.W.Y.

G.E.C.Y.

S.M.Y.

JAMES Z.

T.O.Z.

X. X. X.

1881.

1883

1884

&

FINIS.

Indexes

Index of Names and Devices

Agnes, 143
Albert, 4
Alice, 3, 144
Alpha and Omega, 33(3)
Alphabet, 1
Amélie, 5, 104
&, 212
Andrew, Saint, 34(1)
Annie, 146
Austria, crown of archduke, 23
Austria, crown of, 9

Barons, helmet of, 35(5)
Bastards, helmet of, 35(9)
Belgian Baron, crown of, 12
Belgian Count, crown of, 28
Bella, 148
Benjamin D., 155
Berthe, 7
Betsy, 148

Cardinal-Bishop-Count, coats of arms, 34(2)
Carrie, 154
Catherine, 8
Celia, 152
Charlemagne, 5, 28
Charles of Austria, 9
Charles the Bald, bible of, 33(8, 9); crown of, 5
Chrismon, Christ, 33(2, 3, 4, 5, 6)
City Crests, 15, 20, 21
Claire, 104
Claud, 154
Clotilde, 104
Cora R., 194

Count, crown of, 13
Cousins and Nephews, crown of, 17
Crowns of: Austria, 9, 23; Belgium, 12, 28; England, 12, 16, 17, 20, 25, 26; France, 12, 30; Germany, 12, 31; Hanover, 26; Holy Roman Empire, 3, 23, 24; Hungary, 18; Lombardy, 29; Lorraine, 26; Netherlands, 28; Normandy, 26; Russia, 3, 25, 31; Poland, 27; Persia, 31; Sweden, 12; Tuscany, 31
Czarevitch, crown of, 31

Dates, 1881, 1883, 1884, 212
David, 10, 156
Doges of Venice, 29
Don Q., 192
Dora, 156
Doves, Eucharistic, 33(3)
Dukes, helmet of, 35(2)
Dukes and Peers of England, crown of, 25
Dukes of Lorraine, crown of, 26
Duke William of Normandy, crown of, 26

Edith, 160
Edouard, 12
1881–1884, 212
Eliza, 159
Elizabeth, 13
Emily, 160
Emperor, helmet of, 35(1)
England, crowns of, 16, 25, 26; heraldry of, 19
English Baron, crown of, 12
English Count, crown of, 20
Eudes, see Odo
Eugénie, 104

Evaline, 160
Evangelists, 34(5, 6, 7, 8)

Faith, Hope, Charity, 33(2)
Fanny, 162
Finis, 212
Flora, 163
France, crown of, 30
Frances H. B., 149
Frédéric, 14
French Baron, crown of, 12

Gaston, 15
Gentlemen, helmet of, 35(7)
George, 164
Georges, 16
Gerald, 165
German Baron, crown of, 12
German Empire, crown of, 31
Gertie, 165
Gospels, 34(4)

Hannah, 169
Hanover, crown of, 26
Harry, 168
Hat of Dignity, 25
Hattie, 169
Havre, Le, crest of, 20
Helen G, 169
Hélène, 104
Helmets, 35
Holy Roman Empire, crown of, 3; crown of count, 24;
    crown of prince, 23
Hungary, crown of, 18
Hyacinthe, 17

Isaac, 170
Isidore, 18

Jack, 173
James S., 172
James Z., 212
Jane, 19, 191
Janet, 172
Jeanne, 104
Jessie, 173
Jesus and Mary, 106
Jesus Christ, 33(2)(5)(6)(7)
Joe, 173
John, 173

John, saint, 34(8)
J. Smith, 197
Joseph, 33(9)
Julia, 173

Kate, 174
Katherine, 175
Keys, 34(1)
Kings, helmet of, 35(1)
Knights, helmet of, 35(6)

Larri, 32(4)
Lennox, 177
Léonie, 20
Lewis, 176
Lily, 177
Lizzie, 178
Lombard Kings, crown of, 29
Lottie, 178
Loui, 177
Louis, 21
Louis IX, 8
Louis Philippe, 14
Louisa, 176
Lucy, 179
Luke, Saint, 34(6)
Luxembourg, 22

Marguerite, 24
Maria, 104
Marie, 104, 105
Mark, Saint, 34(7)
Marquis, helmet of, 35(3)
Marquis, heraldry of, 13
Marthe, 104
Mary, St., 33(1)(8)
Mary, 180
Mary Y., 210
Mathilde, 104
Mathilde, Empress, 23
Matthew, Saint, 34(5)
Maud, 183
May, 182
Middle Ages, monogram styles of, 32
Moses, 34(3)

Naval symbol, 15
Nelly, 186
Netherlands, crown of knights, 28
Nettie, 184
New Testament, 34(4)

Nicolas, 25
Nîmes, crest of, 20
Nobility, crown of, 6; helmet of, 35(8)
Nora, 186
Numbers 1881–84, 212

Odo (Eudes) of Aquitaine, crown of, 8
Old Testament, 34(3)
Oliver, 187
Olympe, 26
Oswald, 187
Ottoman, viceroys and princes of, 31

Paris, crest of, 21
Passion, instruments of, 33(4)
Paul, 191
Pearl, 191
Peter, 189
Pierre, 27
Poland, crown of, 27
Pope Léo XIII, 34(1)
Prince, crown of, 23
Princes, helmet of, 35(2)

Queen's children (English), crown of, 17

Ralph, 195
Recuerdo, 106
Renaissance, monogram styles of, 32
Robert, 28
Rome, ancient crown of, 29
Rosa, 193
Rosine, 32(5)
Russia, crown of, 3; crown of grand dukes, 25

Saints, see individual Saints
Sarah, 198
Sebastien, 29
Semper, 106
Shah of Persia, crown of, 31
Smith, J., 197
Sophie, 29
Sovereign Prince, crown of, 23; helmet of, 35(2)
Stephen, 199
Susan, 196
Suzanne, 29
Swedish Baron, crown of, 12

Tablets of Moses, 34(3)
Theodore, 30
Theresa, 201
Thérésa, 104
Timothy, 201
Tom, 203
Trinity, Holy, 33(7)
Tuscany, crown of grand dukes, 31

Vernon, 206
Versailles, crest of, 21
Victor, 32(2)
Vidame, crown of, 13
Virginia, 205
Virginie, 31
Virgin Mary, see Mary, St.
Viscount, helmet of, 35(4); crown of, 7
Vivian, 205

Willie, 208
William of Normandy, crown of, 26
Winnie, 207

Index of Monograms and Ciphers

A A, 3, 41, 103, 111, 112
A A A, 144
A A S, 198
A A S A, 143
A B, 3, 41, 105, 112
A B L, 176
A B Y, 210
A C, 3, 41, 112
A C B, 105, 112
A C C, 152
A C D, 156
A D, 3, 42, 112
A D B, 148
A D G T, 200
A D J, 172
A E, 3, 42, 112
A E A, 143
A E I, 106, 112
A E L, 105, 112
A E O U, 204
A E S, 199
A F, 3, 42, 112
A F L, 177
A F T, 201
A G, 3, 42, 43, 112
A G H M, 180
A G K, 174
A G N, 185
A G P, 190
A G R, 195
A G W, 206
A G Y, 210, 211
A H, 3, 43, 112
A H F, 161
A H L, 176
A H M, 181

A H R, 195
A I, 3, 43, 112
A J, 3, 43, 112
A J D, 155, 157
A J M, 182
A J Y, 211
A K, 3, 43, 44, 112
A K E, 158
A L, 3, 44, 112, 137, 176
A L V, 205
A M, 4, 44, 106, 112
A McE, 158
A & M D, 155
A M M Y, 210
A M N, 186
A M P, 190
A M Y, 211
A N, 4, 44, 112
A N D, 112
A N G, 166
A N W, 208
A O, 4, 45, 112
A O K, 175
A O S, 198
A O W, 207, 208
A P, 4, 45, 112
A P T, 202
A P V, 205
A Q, 4, 45, 112
A R, 4, 45, 112
A R K, 174
A R S, 197
A & R W, 209
A S, 4, 45, 46, 112
A S O, 188
A S Q, 192

A S S, 196
A S T, 203
A S Y, 211
A T, 4, 46, 112
A T G, 166
A T H, 169
A T M, 180
A T U, 204
A U, 4, 46, 112
A V, 4, 46, 112
A V F W, 206
A V M, 182
A W, 4, 46, 112
A W S, 197
A X, 4, 46, 112
A Y, 5, 46, 112
A Y M, 180
A Z, 5, 46, 112
A—Z, 1

B A, 105, 113
B A W & Co, 206
B B, 5, 47, 111, 113
B B 1880, 147
B C, 5, 47, 113
B C B, 149
B C D D, 155
B C E, 159
B C L, 178
B C P, 123
B D, 5, 47, 111, 113
B de Q, 192
B D F, 162
B E, 5, 47, 48, 113
B E B I, 170

B E C, 152
B E G, 164
B F, 5, 48, 113
B F & Co, 163
B F P, 189
B F U, 204
B G, 5, 48, 113
B G C, 152
B G I, 171
B G R, 194
B H, 5, 48, 49, 113
B I, 5, 49, 113
B J, 5, 49, 113
B J S, 196
B K, 5, 49, 113
B L, 6, 49, 113
B M, 6, 50, 113
B N, 6, 50, 113
B N H, 167
B N O, 113
B O, 6, 50, 113
B O E T, 203
B O M, 183
B P, 6, 51, 113
B Q, 6, 51, 113
B R, 6, 51, 113
B R S, 197
B S, 6, 51, 113
B S R, 193
B T, 6, 52, 113
B U, 6, 52, 113
B V, 6, 52, 113
B W, 6, 52, 113
B X, 7, 52, 113
B Y, 7, 52, 113
B Z, 7, 52, 113

C, 136
C A, 114
C A B, 149
C A F, 161
C A H H, 167
C A M, 180
C A R, 114
C B, 114, 119
C B E A, 144
C B I, 171
C C, 7, 53, 114, 118
C C C, 53, 111
C C C T, 200
C C S, 197
C D, 7, 53, 114
C D B, 148
C E, 7, 53, 54, 114

C E D, 156
C E D I, 170
C E G, 154, 165
C E O, 188
C E S, 128
C E W, 206
C F, 7, 54, 114
C F T, 200
C G, 7, 54, 114
C G F A, 145
C G J I, 171
C H, 7, 54, 114
C H D, 156
C H F, 162
C H K, 175
C I, 7, 54, 55, 114
C J, 7, 55, 114
C J A, 145
C J C R, 195
C K, 7, 55, 114
C K B, 149
C K S, 198
C K Y M, 182
C L, 7, 55, 114
C M, 7, 55, 56, 114
C M T, 200
C N, 8, 56, 114
C O, 8, 56, 114
C P, 8, 56, 57, 114
C Q, 8, 57, 114
C R, 8, 57, 114
C R M, 181
C S, 8, 57, 105, 114
C S B, 149
C T, 8, 58, 114
C T R, 194
C U, 8, 58, 114
C V, 8, 58, 114
C W, 8, 58, 114
C W B, 150
C X, 8, 58, 114, 120
C Y, 8, 58, 114
C Z, 9, 58, 114

D, 9
D A, 115
D B, 115
D B E, 160
D C, 115
D C E, 160
D D, 9, 59, 111, 115
D D F H, 167
D E, 9, 59, 115
D E C, 153

D E J, 173
D E K, 175
D F, 9, 59, 115
D F A, 146
D G, 9, 59, 60, 115
D G K, 174
D G M, 183
D H, 9, 60, 115
D H T, 203
D I, 9, 60, 115
D J, 9, 60, 61, 115
D K, 9, 61, 115
D L, 9, 61, 115
D L T C, 152
D M, 9, 61, 115
D McC, 152
D M M, 182
D N, 9, 62, 115
D O, 9, 62, 115
D P, 9, 62, 115
D Q, 10, 62, 115
D R, 10, 62, 63, 115
D S, 10, 63, 115
D S F, 115
D S McE, 158
D S O F, 163
D T, 10, 63, 115
D T N, 184
D U, 10, 63, 115
D V, 10, 64, 115
D W, 10, 64, 115
D X, 10, 64, 115
D Y, 10, 64, 115
D Z, 10, 64, 115

E, 10, 115
E A, 116
E B, 116
E B N, 186
E C, 116
E C B, 149
E C C, 153
E C E, 158
E C M, 183
E C McD, 156
E C N, 186
E C T, 132
E D, 116
E D G, 164
E D H, 168
E E, 62, 111, 116, 128
E F, 10, 65, 116
E F J, 173
E F Q, 192

E G, 11, 65, 116
E G C, 154
E G H, 167
E G I, 171
E & G M, 183
E H, 11, 65, 116
E H A, 144
E H F, 163
E H L, 178
E I, 11, 65, 116
E I H, 168
E I U, 204
E J, 11, 66, 116
E J E, 159
E J L, 177
E K, 11, 66, 116
E K W, 209
E L, 11, 66, 116
E L D, 157
E L F, 162
E L J, 172
E L P, 190
E M, 11, 66, 116
E M B S, 198
E N, 11, 67, 116
E N A, 143
E N N, 186
E O, 11, 67, 116
E P, 11, 67, 116
E Q, 11, 67, 116
E R, 12, 67, 68, 116
E R W, 206
E S, 12, 68
E S G, 165
E S R, 193
E S T, 202
E T, 12, 68, 116
E T A, 143
E T C, 151
E T K, 175
E T S W, 208
E T T, 200
E U, 12, 68, 116
E V, 12, 68, 116
E W, 12, 69, 116, 126
E X, 12, 69, 116
E Y, 12, 69, 116
E Z, 12, 69, 116

F A, 117
F A G, 164
F B, 117
F C, 117
F D, 117

F D L, 178
F E, 117
F E D, 155
F E O, 187
F F, 69, 111, 117
F G, 13, 69, 117
F G D W, 207
F G O, 188
F H, 13, 70, 117
F I, 13, 70, 117
F J, 13, 70, 117
F J S, 196
F K, 13, 70, 117, 125
F L, 13, 70, 117
F L M, 182
F M, 13, 71, 117
F M H, 169
F N, 13, 71, 117
F N D, 157
F N H W, 209
F O, 13, 71, 117
F P, 13, 71, 117
F Q, 13, 72, 117
F R, 13, 72, 117
F S, 14, 32, 72, 117
F T, 14, 72, 117
F T G, 165
F U, 14, 72, 117
F V, 14, 73, 117
F W, 14, 73, 117
F X, 14, 73, 117
F Y, 14, 73, 117
F Z, 14, 73, 117

G, 14
G A, 118
G A A W, 207
G A C R, 195
G A L, 177
G A M, 181, 183
G A Y, 210
G B, 118
G and B, 150
G C, 118
G C A, 146
G C F, 162
G C L, 176
G C P W, 206
G C T, 202
G D, 111, 118
G E, 103, 118
G E C Y, 211
G E P, 189
G F, 118

G F B, 147
G F H, 167
G F T, 203
G G, 71, 111
G G I, 170
G G S, 196
G H, 14, 74, 118
G H E, 159
G H F L, 178
G H N, 185
G H P, 191
G H R, 141
G I, 14, 74, 118
G I D, 157
G I E, 160
G I R, 118
G J, 14, 74, 118
G J A, 143
G J F, 163
G J L V, 205
G K, 15, 74, 118
G K F A, 146
G L, 15, 74, 118
G L H R, 195
G L N H, 168
G M, 15, 75, 118
G M S, 199
G M T, 202
G N, 15, 75, 118
G O, 15, 75, 118
G P, 15, 75, 118
G Q, 15, 76, 118
G R, 15, 76, 118
G R C Y, 210
G R F, 161
G S, 15, 76, 118
G S M, 180
G S P, 190
G S U, 204
G T, 15, 76, 118
G T O A, 146
G U, 15, 76, 118
G V, 16, 76, 118
G W, 16, 77, 118
G X, 16, 77, 118
G Y, 16, 77, 118
G Y N, 185
G Z, 16, 77, 118

H, 16
H A, 119
H A H, 167
H A T, 200
H B, 119

H B J, 105
H B P, 191
H C, 119
H C & Co, 153
H C B, 148
H C S, 197
H D, 115
H D G I, 171
H D O, 188
H E N M, 180
H F, 119
H F L, 179
H F M, 182
H G, 119
H G N, 184
H G U, 204
H H, 77, 103, 105, 111, 119
H I, 16, 77, 119
H I B, 119
H J, 16, 77, 119
H K, 16, 78, 119
H L, 16, 78, 119
H L I, 170
H M, 16, 78, 119
H M C, 154
H M I, 136
H M J, 173
H N, 16, 78, 119
H N F, 161
H N H, 168
H O, 16, 78, 119
H O S, 199
H P, 16, 79, 119
H Q, 17, 79, 119
H R, 17, 79, 105, 119
H S, 17, 79, 119
H S L, 179
H S T, 202
H T, 17, 79, 119
H & T, 201
H T P, 189
H U, 17, 79, 119
H V, 17, 80, 119
H W, 17, 80, 119
H W E, 160
H W Y, 211
H X, 17, 80, 119
H Y, 18, 80, 119
H Z, 18, 80, 119

I, 18
I A, 120
I A E P, 190
I A G, 32(1)

I A J, 172
I A M, 181
I B, 120
I B B, 150
I B O B, 147
I C, 120
I D, 120, 135
I D C, 154
I E, 120
I E E, 160
I E V W, 207
I F, 120
I G, 120
I G K, 175
I G O O, 188
I G R, 194
I H, 120
I H E, 159
I H S, 106, 196
I H W, 114, 117
I I, 18, 80, 111, 120
I J, 18, 80, 120
I K, 18, 80, 120
I L, 18, 80, 81, 120
I M, 18, 81, 106, 120
I M C, 127
I M H M, 181
I M O, 187
I N, 18, 81, 120
I N R I, 106
I O, 18, 81, 120
I O S, 198
I P, 18, 81, 120
I Q, 18, 81, 120
I R, 18, 81, 120, 129
I R S, 199
I S, 18, 81, 120
I S A, 171
I S D, 113
I S K, 174
I S S, 199
I T, 18, 82, 120
I U, 18, 82, 120
I V, 18, 82, 120
I W, 19, 82, 120
I X, 19, 82, 120
I Y, 19, 82, 120
I Z, 19, 82, 120

J, 19
J A, 19
J A A, 146
J A C B, 150
J A K, 174

J A L, 176
J A P, 189
J A S C, 152
J B, 121
J B C K, 174
J B E, 159
J B F, 161
J B V, 205
J C, 121
J C J T, 200
J C S, 197
J C S G, 166
J C V, 205
J C W, 209
J D, 121
J D O G, 166
J E, 121
J E C, 121, 151
J E D O, 187
J E J S, 197
J E L, 179
J E L S, 197
J E N, 186
J E N O, 187
J E R, 193, 195
J E W, 208
J F, 121
J F D G, 164
J F F O, 188
J G, 121
J G F, 161, 162
J G M, 181
J G P, 189
J G R, 193
J G W, 206
J G Y, 210
J H, 121
J H A, 143
J H L G, 166
J H M, 181
J H M F, 162
J I, 121
J J, 19, 82, 111, 121
J J G, 166
J K, 19, 83, 121
J L, 19, 83, 121
J L B, 121
J M, 19, 83, 121, 135
J M B, 148
J McL, 177
J M W A, 144
J N, 19, 83, 121
J O, 19, 83, 121
J O A, 144
J O S, 198

J O Y, 211
J P, 19, 83, 84, 121
J P H, 168
J P T, 201
J Q, 19, 84, 121
J R, 20, 84, 121
J & R, 193
J R K, 175
J S, 20, 84, 121
J S M, 182
J S N, 185
J S Q, 192
J T, 20, 84, 121
J T B, 147
J T S, 199
J T W, 208
J U, 20, 84, 121
J U E, 158
J V, 20, 84, 85, 121
J W, 20, 85, 121
J W H, 169
J W P, 190
J X, 20, 85, 121
J Y, 20, 85, 121
J Z, 20, 85, 121

K, 20
K A, 122
K B, 122
K C, 122
K C T, 200
K D, 122
K E, 122
K F, 122
K G, 122
K H, 122
K H McE, 160
K I, 122
K I N, 122
K J, 122
K K, 85, 111, 122
K L, 20, 85, 122
K M, 20, 85, 86, 122
K M F, 122
K M L, 177
K N, 20, 86, 122
K O, 21, 86, 122
K P, 21, 86, 122
K Q, 21, 86, 122
K R, 21, 86, 122
K S, 21, 87, 122
K S B, 150
K T, 21, 87, 122
K T D, 157

K T G, 165
K T I, 170
K U, 21, 87, 122
K V, 21, 87, 122
K W, 21, 87, 122
K X, 21, 87, 122
K Y, 21, 87, 122
K Z, 21, 87, 122

L, 22
L A, 123
L A D, 123
L A F, 163
L B, 123
L C, 123
L D, 123
L E, 123
L E B, 150
L E C, 151
L E R O, 187
L F, 123
L G D, 157
L H, 123
L H A P, 190
L I, 123
L J, 22, 123
L K, 22, 123
L K N G, 164
L L, 22, 88, 111, 123
L M, 22, 88, 123
L M W, 209
L N, 22, 88, 123
L N F, 161
L O, 22, 88, 123
L P, 22, 88, 89, 123
L Q, 22, 89, 123
L R, 22, 89, 123
L R B C, 153
L S, 22, 89, 123
L T, 22, 89, 123
L U, 22, 89, 123
L U T, 203
L V, 22, 89, 90, 123
L W, 22, 90, 123
L X, 23, 90, 123
L Y, 23, 90, 123
L Z, 23, 90, 123

M A, 105, 124
M A B, 147
M A D, 155
M A D C, 151
M A E, 158

M A K, 175
M A M, 181
M A M L, 179
M A R, 193
M A V, 205
M B, 124
M B A, 144
M B D, 155
M C, 124
M & C, 153
M C A, 143
McC, 151
M C I, 170
M C L, 178
M C M R, 193
M C W, 206
M D, 124
M D W, 207
M E, 124
M E A, 143
M E G, 165
M E I, 171
M E N, 124, 184
M E P, 189
M E S D, 156
M F, 124
M F M F, 161
M G, 124
M G C, 154
M H, 124
M I, 124
M I N, 185
M J, 124
M K, 124
M L, 124
M L & Co, 177
M L B, 150
M L F, 161
M M, 23, 90, 103, 105, 111, 124
M M T, 200
M N, 23, 90, 124
M N D, 157
M O, 23, 90, 91, 124
M O N T, 203
M P, 23, 91, 124, 134
M Q, 23, 91, 124
M R, 23, 91, 105, 124
M R F, 162
M S, 23, 91, 124
M & S, 197
M S R, 195
M T, 23, 91, 124
M & T, 201
M T E, 158
M U, 23, 91, 124

M U R, 194
M V, 24, 92, 124
M V E, 159
M W, 24, 92, 124
M W A O, 187
M X, 24, 92, 124
M Y, 24, 92, 124
M Z, 24, 92, 124

N, 24
N A, 125
N A U, 204
N B, 125
N C, 125
N D, 125
N E, 125
N E D H, 169
N E G, 125
N E S A, 145
N F, 125
N F Y, 210
N G, 125
N G B, 149
N H, 125
N H M, 183
N H M B, 148
N I, 125
N J, 125
N K, 125
N L, 125
N M, 125
N M E Q, 192
N N, 24, 92, 111, 125
N O, 24, 92, 125
N O C B, 147
N P, 24, 92, 125
N Q, 24, 93, 125
N R, 24, 93, 125
N S, 24, 93, 125
N S C, 153
N T, 24, 93, 125
N U, 25, 93, 125
N V, 25, 93, 125
N W, 25, 93, 125
N X, 25, 94, 125
N Y, 25, 94, 125
N Z, 25, 94, 125

O, 25, 32(4)
O A, 126
O B, 126
O B B, 148
O C, 126

O C G, 166
O D, 126
O E, 126
O E G B, 147
O F, 126
O G, 126
O G F, 163
O H, 126
O H D, 157
O I, 126
O J, 126
O K, 126
O L, 126
O la K, 174
O M, 103, 126
O M F, 126
O M O, 188
O M P, 190
O N, 126
O N H K, 174
O O, 92, 111, 126
O P, 25, 94, 126
O Q, 25, 94, 126
O R, 25, 94, 124
O S, 25, 94, 126
O S B, 148
O S G T, 201
O S O S, 196
O S R, 194
O T, 25, 95, 126
O U, 26, 95, 126
O V, 26, 95, 126
O W, 26, 95, 126
O X, 26, 95, 126
O Y, 26, 95, 126
O Z, 26, 95, 126

P, 26
P A, 127
P A S, 197
P B, 127
P C, 127
P C A, 146
P D, 127
P D C, 152
P E, 127
P E C, 153
P F, 127
P G, 127
P G H N, 184
P G L, 176
P H, 127
P H M, 180
P H W, 209

P I, 127
P J, 127
P J B, 150
P K, 127
P L, 127
P L G, 165
P M, 127
P N, 127
P O, 127
P P, 95, 111, 127
P Q, 26, 96, 127
P R, 26, 96, 127
P S, 26, 96, 127
P T, 26, 96, 127
P U, 26, 96, 127
P V, 26, 96, 97, 127
P W, 27, 97, 127
P X, 27, 97, 127
P Y, 27, 97, 127
P Z, 27, 97, 127

Q, 27
Q A, 128
Q B, 128
Q C, 128
Q D, 128
Q E, 128
Q E R V B, 192
Q F, 128
Q G, 128
Q H, 128
Q I, 128
Q J, 128
Q K, 128
Q L, 128
Q M, 128
Q N, 128
Q O, 128
Q P, 128
Q Q, 97, 111, 128
Q R, 27, 97, 128
Q S, 27, 97, 128
Q T, 27, 97, 128
Q U, 27, 97, 128
Q V, 27, 98, 128
Q W, 27, 98, 128
Q X, 28, 98, 128
Q Y, 28, 98, 128
Q Z, 28, 98, 128

R, 28
R A, 129
R A & Co, 145

R A E, 116
R A H, 169
R A & J H, 168
R B, 129
R C, 129
R C M, 183
R C S, 198
R D, 129
R D W, 208
R E, 129
R E H Q, 192
R F, 129
R G, 129
R G N, 185
R H, 129
R I, 129
R J, 129
R K, 129
R L, 129
R M, 129
R McF, 163
R McQ, 192
R N, 129
R O, 129
R P, 129
R Q, 129
R R, 28, 98, 111, 124, 129
R S, 28, 98, 129
R S M, 181
R T, 28, 99, 129
R U, 28, 99, 129
R V, 28, 99, 129
R V T, 203
R W, 28, 99, 129
R X, 28, 99, 129
R Y, 29, 99, 129
R Z, 29, 99, 129

S, 29
S A, 130
S A D, 157
S A G, 165
S A H, 167
S A P, 191
S B, 103, 130
S B G C, 151
S B N, 184
S B S I, 171
S B T, 202
S C, 130
S C E, 158
S C I, 171
S C J, 172
S C O W, 208

S C P, 191
S C W, 206, 208
S D, 105, 130
S D G, 166
S E, 130
S E L, 176
S F, 130
S G, 130
S G A, 145
S G B, 150
S G F, 163
S G O, 187
S G T, 202
S H, 130
S I, 130
S I N, 185
S J, 130
S K, 130
S L, 111, 130
S & L, 179
S L A, 144
S M, 130
S McT, 201
S M L, 176
S M W, 130
S M Y, 211
S N, 130
S O, 130
S P, 130
S P C, 154
S Q, 130
S R, 130
S S, 99, 130
S S D, 156
S T, 29, 100, 130
St. A, 145
St. A B B, 151
St. E C C, 152
St. G, 164
St. N, 186
St. P, 191
S U, 29, 100, 130
S V, 29, 100, 130
S W, 29, 100, 130
S X, 30, 100, 130
S Y, 30, 100, 130
S Y & Co, 211
S Z, 30, 100, 130

T, 30
T A, 131
T A D, 157
T & A H, 167
T A N, 185

T A T, 203
T B, 131
T B A, 145
T C, 131
T C C, 153
T C F, 161
T C J, 172
T C K, 174
T D, 131
T D L, 178
T E, 131
T E D, 156
T E H, 167
T E M, 132
T E N, 184
T E O, 188
T E S W, 207
T F, 131
T F A W, 207
T F S, 199
T G, 131
T G F, 162
T G J, 172
T G K, 175
T H, 131
T H A, 145
T H N, 186
T I, 131
T J, 131
T J H, 169
T J McK, 174
T J O, 188
T K, 131
T L, 131
T L A, 143
T L B, 131
T L G, 166
T M, 131
T M L, 179
T M McB, 149
T N, 131
T O, 131
T O N, 184
T O Z, 212
T P, 131
T Q, 131
T R, 129, 131
T R E, 159
T R N, 185
T S, 131
T S A, 143
T S B, 147
T S I, 170
T S L, 179
T S R, 193

T S U, 204
T T, 30, 100, 111, 131
T T R, 194
T U, 30, 101, 131
T U H R, 194
T U S, 196
T V, 30, 101, 131
T V W, 209
T W, 30, 101, 131
T X, 30, 101, 131
T Y, 30, 101, 131
T Y W, 209
T Z, 30, 101, 131

U, 30
U A, 132
U B, 132
U C, 132
U C L, 178
U D, 132
U E, 132
U F, 132
U G, 132
U H, 132
U I, 132
U J, 132
U K, 132
U L, 132
U M, 132
U N, 132
U O, 132
U O U R, 194
U P, 132
U Q, 132
U R, 132
U S, 132
U S E, 159
U T, 132
U U, 30, 101, 111, 132
U V, 30, 101, 132
U W, 31, 101, 132
U X, 31, 101, 132
U Y, 31, 101, 132
U Z, 31, 102, 132

V, 133
V A, 133
V A D, 133
V B, 133
V C, 133
V D, 133
V E, 133
V F, 133

V G, 133
V G A, 144
V H, 133
V I, 133
V J, 133
V K, 133
V L, 133
V M, 133
V M A, 146
V M L, 179
V N, 133
V O, 133
V O C, 151
V P, 133
V Q, 133
V R, 133
V S, 133
V T, 133
V U, 133
V V, 31, 102, 111, 133
V W, 31, 102, 133
V X, 31, 102, 133
V Y, 31, 102, 133
V Z, 31, 102, 133

W, 137
W A, 135
W A C, 164
W A P, 189
W A S, 199
W A W, 209
W B, 134
W B S, 196
W C, 134
W D, 134
W E, 134
W E A, 145
W E B, 147
W E B G L, 176
W E S, 198
W F, 134
W F A, 146
W G, 134
W G A C, 153
W G P, 191
W H, 134
W H B, 149
W H O, 134
W H W, 207
W I, 134
W I N, 184
W I U, 204
W J, 134
W J A, 143

W J M, 183
W J & Co, 173
W K, 134
W L, 134
W M, 134
W M P, 190
W M S T, 202
W N, 134
W N Y, 210
W O, 134
W O A, 143
W P, 134
W P I, 170
W Q, 134
W R, 134
W S, 134
W S D, 155
W S F, 161
W T, 131, 134
W T G, 164
W T M, 180
W U, 134
W V, 134
W W, 31, 102, 111, 134
W W M, 182
W X, 31, 134
W Y, 31, 134
W Z, 31, 102, 134

X A, 135
X B, 135
X C, 135
X D, 135
X E, 135
X F, 135
X G, 135
X H, 135
X I, 135
X J, 135
X K, 135
X L, 135
X M, 135
X N, 135
X O, 135
X P, 135
X Q, 135
X R, 135
X S, 135
X T, 135
X U, 135
X V, 135
X W, 102, 135
X X, 31, 103, 111, 135
X X X, 212

X Y, 31, 103, 135
X Z, 31, 103, 135

Y A, 136
Y A T, 201
Y B, 136
Y C, 136
Y D, 136
Y E, 136
Y F, 136
Y G, 136
Y G H, 168
Y H, 136
Y I, 136
Y J, 136
Y K, 136
Y L, 136
Y M, 136
Y N, 136

Y O, 136
Y P, 136
Y Q, 136
Y R, 136
Y S, 136
Y T, 136
Y U, 136
Y V, 136
Y W, 102, 136
Y X, 136
Y Y, 31, 103, 111, 136
Y Z, 31, 103, 136

Z A, 137
Z B, 137
Z C, 137
Z D, 137
Z E, 137
Z F, 137

Z G, 137
Z H, 137
Z I, 137
Z J, 137
Z K, 137
Z L, 137
Z M, 137
Z N, 137
Z O, 137
Z P, 137
Z Q, 137
Z R, 137
Z S, 137
Z T, 137
Z U, 137
Z V, 137
Z W, 137
Z X, 137
Z Y, 137
Z Z, 103, 111, 137